BIG NOISE
FROM A
WEE
COUNTRY

First published 2011 by Noisewave.

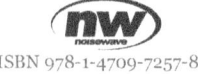

ISBN 978-1-4709-7257-8

www.martinkielty.com

Introduction

Big Noise was the fanzine I ran throughout the 1990s. Some zines follow a particular band, or a genre, or a political movement. I was interested in what made Scotland's rock'n'roll different from everyone else's. I was always sure it *was* different – interviews with a wide variety of Scots artists and an equal range of folk from elsewhere only supported my belief.

This book isn't just named after the zine – it's a new edition, which I admit I would never have got away with photocopying while the boss thought I was working late. And you can't have one for free. And you can't get your band in it. And I'm not going to harass you to write something for it.

So get strapped in: this is a rollercoaster ride. We're gonna start fast and zoom through history at a speed you wouldn't believe. Along the way we'll sneak down a couple of sidestreets and peak behind the odd set of curtains, but for most of the trip it's gonna be splat-*splat*-**splat** as we whistle-stop through fifty years of action and adventure. Jazz, skiffle, beat, prog, glam, pop, twee, dance and crossover will all make an appearance. But only for a moment, because we're moving at intergalactic velocities.

There's no way I could fit everything in, and I didn't want to try. What I did want to do, though, is what I always try to do: tell stories which share the passion and magic I've discovered underneath what some people think is nothing more than a £5-billion-per-year business.

People get bored reading official history when it's just a list of kings and battles. In the same way, this isn't just a list of rock stars and hit records – it's about the *real* history, the *real* people and the *real* stories.

Ready? Here we go...

MARTIN KIELTY

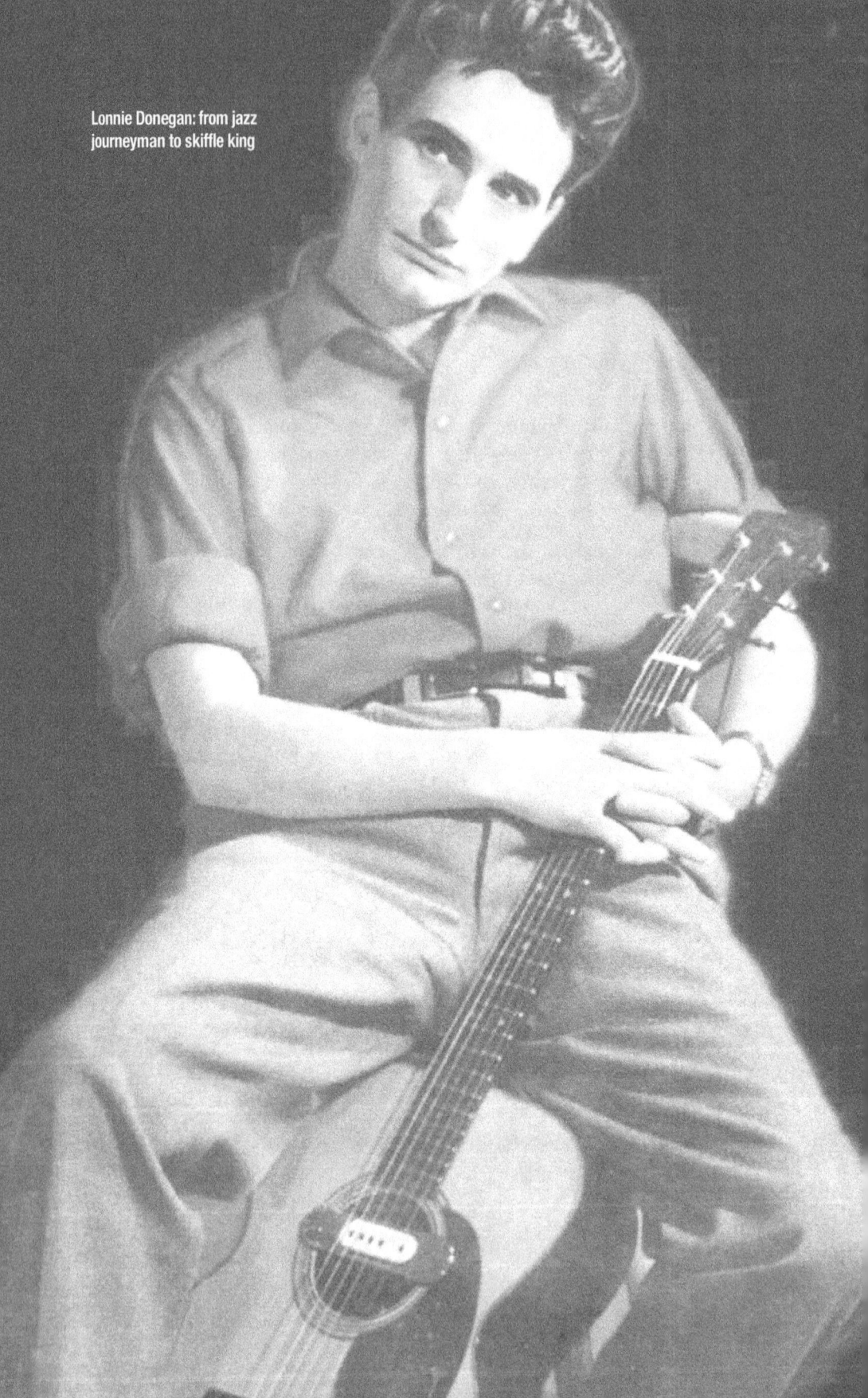

Lonnie Donegan: from jazz journeyman to skiffle king

Scotland's first punk

Lonnie Donegan and the music everyone could play

IN 1956 a top ten-hit changed popular music for ever. Its performer's name was Lonnie Donegan, his track was a cover of Leadbelly's Rock Island Line, and he invented skiffle. Within weeks the whole world was joining in.

The first charts of 1956 (which had only recently begun listing by record sales instead of sheet-music ones) included Frank Sinatra's *Love and Marriage*, Frank Sinatra's *Love is The Tender Trap*, Gary Miller's *Robin Hood*, Dick James' *Robin Hood*, Bill Hayes' *Ballad of Davy Crockett*, Tennessee Ernie Ford's *Ballad of Davy Crockett*, and Tennessee Ernie Ford's *Sixteen Tons*. 'One singer one song' came later, it seems.

The hit parade represented high-falutin' romantic croonings, light-hearted ditties, boys' own TV show themes and even Ernie's workin' class dirges – but Lonnie's offering was completely new. That's because anyone could play it.

He didn't actually have a tea-chest bass (that came later), but he did have the banjo and the washboard, a had a vocal delivery like you and me (if we were pretending to be American, of course) and he played the tune in a simplistic three-chord style. If folk like Elvis and Bill Haley had captured the mood of a generation, Glasgow-born Lonnie had given everyone a crash course in the language.

CHAS McDEVITT, Chas McDevitt Skiffle Group**:** I blame George Formby, actually – so much music just after the war was dull as dishwater. Even though his stuff had been recorded in the 1930s it made us realise music could be made very easily – and it could be bright and cheery too.

PETER McCRAE: It really did happen overnight. My dad had a guitar and he was chuffed I was showing an interest – but I think he hoped I'd move on from skiffle... As soon as I could play those chords I got a few mates from school round the house. We had three guitars, a tea-chest bass and a washboard, and we could only play Rock Island Line – but in our heads we were already stars!

PETE AGNEW, Nazareth**:** Some school mates and I got together and called our group the Spitfires, and we entered the Fife Under-15 Skiffle Competition at the ABC in Kirkcaldy. It was our very first gig – I was the singer and my mates had their big brothers' acoustic guitars, and they couldn't play one single chord between them. We won the cup! It gives you an idea of the standard of musicianship at the time...

ROY KITLEY: When I was 15 I set up the Pythons Skiffle Group – we cribbed the name from The Vipers, one of the big successful groups of the time. We were kept really busy with cinema gigs, church socials, parties and clubs. Thousands of skiffle groups sprung up from nowhere - often there were several in one street, and rivalry was pretty fierce. Songs like *In The Evening*, *Midnight Special* and *Bury My Body* are still fresh in my mind. Some of the Pythons get back together to play them and they still sound great.

Ted-icated followers
Expensive fashion begins to move north

WHEN THE Teddy Boy fashion was glued to teen-angst movie *The Blackboard Jungle* in London in 1955, the sharp suits and ducks-arse quiff headed north slowly but surely. The style itself was a gluing together of 'spiv' outfits worn by east end scrap merchants and the desire to cheer up drab demob suits. It didn't slice right through Scottish culture the way the papers suggested. While The *Daily Record*'s Pat Roller carried a weekly summary of Teddy terror from coast to coast, in many of Scotland's ballrooms, the bequiffed ones were a minority.

ROLLIN' JOE: I didn't see that many Teds around. There were a few; not Showaddy-waddy Teds, just guys with long jackets, thin trousers, thick brogues shoes, the wee tie, the hair and all. But when you went to the Barrowland in Glasgow, the first thing you saw was people jiving. In the corner – they called it Mug's Alley – there were people who knew what they were doing.

The Teds were just jumping about; they were enjoying themselves but not many of them were any good at jiving. I think if there were all that many Teds in Scotland, most of them were outside the cities. Most of us just wore suits. Anyway, it wasn't about being flash – it was about being smart, dancing and meeting girls.

PAT LEACH: The Ted look arrived in Thurso from Glasgow; some of the boys working on the Dounreay reactor brought the gear up. I liked the look of it but it was 78 bob for a jacket... that was nearly £4, and I was earning less than £6 a week. Still, I saved up and got all the gear, and I remember feeling well flash as I went about.

One Saturday afternoon I passed my dad in the street and he was talking to the local doctor – and he totally blanked me! I was saying, 'Remember me, Dad? Your eldest son?' But he was acting as if I wasn't there. Even the doctor was joining in. I didn't understand – it was just fashion, I didn't go round slashing people or anything. But it was all that old tradition stuff. I still looked great though...

The riot that never was

The anti-teenager media backlash gets into swing

WE CAN SAY with some certainty that the Ricky Barnes All Stars was Scotland's first rock'n'roll band, followed shortly afterwards by acts like Butch and the Bandits, the Saints, the Kinsmen, the Falcons, at least two Crusaders and many more. We can also say the All Stars were responsible for the country's first rock'n'roll riot, and *Tiny Bubbles* crooner Sydney Devine stopped it. It's in the history books... but it's almost certainly bobbins.

BILL ALLISON: Paisley Town Hall was always a favourite with us. Band night was usually Saturday and Jimmy McCracken was a regular, then there was a talent contest on Sunday. That Sunday we had the Ricky Barnes All Stars playing instead.

The hall was all seated except for a space between the front rows and the stage. All the girls used to crowd in there to dance. Their handbags and umbrellas were placed – and I mean *placed* – on the stage. The manager, Mr Edmondson, was a real gentleman and he wasn't bothered. Neither were the bouncers or the bands.

The All Stars did a song called Skin Deep which had a drum solo, and like many bands to this day, the rest of the musicians went off stage while the drummer did his bit. They came back on, finished the set, everyone clapped, and that was that.

Next day I picked up the paper and saw the headline *Riot at Town Hall* across the front page. The article went on about items being thrown onto the stage, but the nearest thing to that was all the umbrellas and bags that had been placed on stage. Then it said the band had walked off in disgust, when they'd just gone off during the drum solo. Sydney Devine? With the passage of time I can't say for certain he wasn't there, but I'm pretty sure there was no one else on the bill beside the All Stars. We did have an eccentric old woman in her seventies, we all called her Granny, who used to sing at the talent contests – very badly! It's more than likely she was screeching away during the interval, but I can't remember.

Music from far away

Rock on the airwaves – if the weather is just right

AS THE rock'n'roll era took hold it wasn't always easy to keep up with the latest developments. The Musicians' Union was campaigning to have the new bands banned because the were putting older established professionals out of work. And there wasn't much chance of hearing the new music on radio either. The BBC continued to broadcast the material they always had. Rock'n'roll wasn't getting a look in – unless the night was still and the sky was cloudy; then maybe, just *maybe*, you could tune into Radio Luxembourg.

LIZ HAYES: Luxembourg was the news channel for anyone who cared about music. You tuned into 208 or 1440 and found this crackly station that played all these magic new tunes you couldn't get in Scotland. You'd go mad for all the American music – and you'd go even madder when you lost the signal and missed the best bit of the song! But that made it all the more magical. You were listening to music from far, far away, and it just fired up your imagination.

I don't think it's as easy to fall in love with a song now as it was then. And it was all about falling in love with songs, not about starting a teenage rebellion. I couldn't even have speled 'rebellion'!

SANDY ALBRIGHT: Sometimes it drove you mental because Luxembourg only played about a minute of each song. Even if you could get the record here there wasn't much chance of being able to afford it. So sometimes you'd just sit, despairing of what you were missing. It was great, though.

ALAN MAIR, The Beatstalkers: Rhythm was in my blood. We lived with my gran, and I loved it when my uncles put Radio Luxembourg on. Even if I was meant to be in bed I couldn't help dancing around if I heard a song I liked. The actual sound of guitars really moved me too. My mum bought me an old acoustic one at an auction and I used to play it with my ear stuck to it, so I could hear a kind of electric sound. But when you got to thirteen or fourteen, and you were just becoming aware of yourself, you realised it was cool to be in a band. That's why everyone was doing it.

Rock comes to Scotland
The American dream hits town

FREDDIE BELL and the Bell Boys was the first bona fide American rock group to play in Scotland. After they presumably took the news back home that us Scots were cool and could rock, the trickle began to become a flood.

CHARLIE GRACIE: I was the first solo American act to tour Britain, and I remember

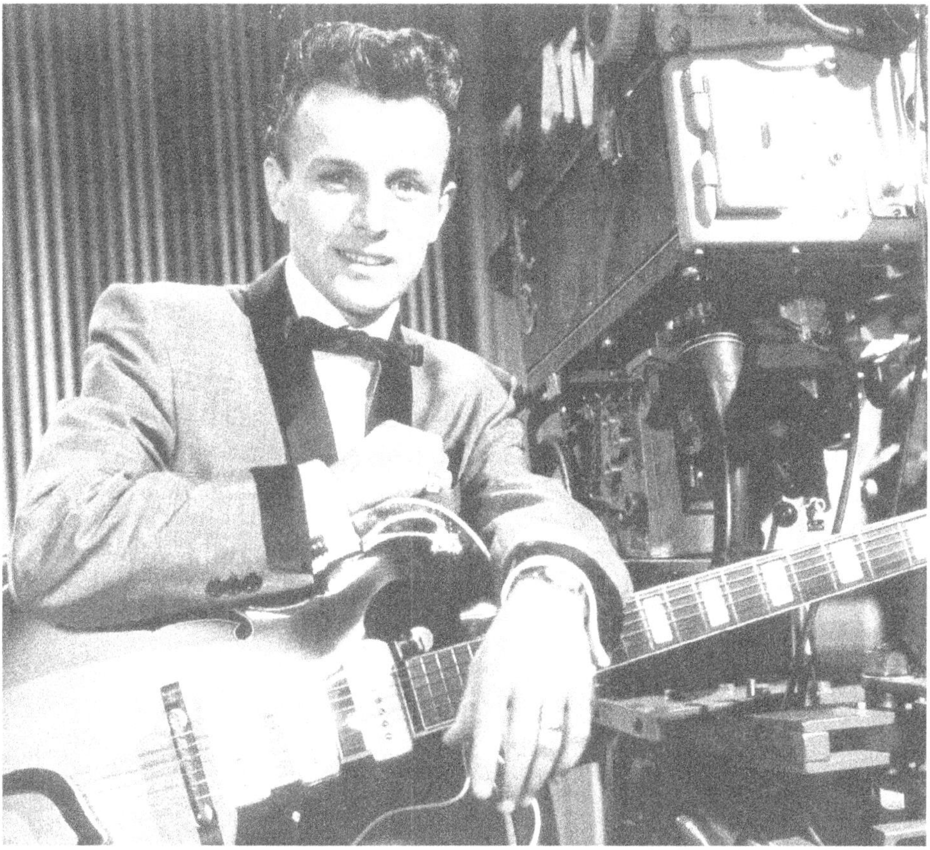

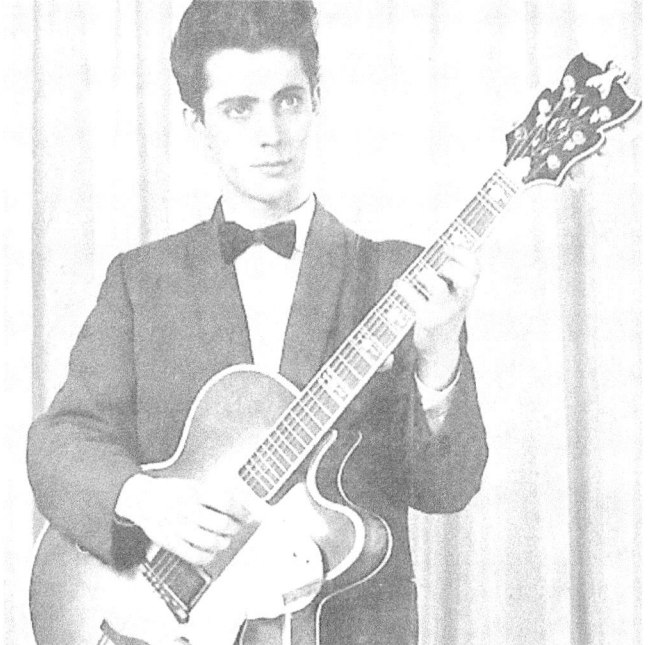

Above: Charlie Gracie, complete with fresh wedding ring, during his first UK tour

Left: Joe Moretti

the Scottish audiences being very warm and passionate. I distinctly recall the welcome I and my new bride received – we'd only been married six weeks. I did two British tours. The first was supposed to last six weeks but Lew and Leslie Grade, who promoted it, extended it to ten.

I was twenty-two and my wife was just eighteen. Imagine what it felt like when we were leaving Glasgow and all these fans turned up at the train station, crying and begging us not to go! We were on the verge of tears too – it was very, very emotional. It was like a scene from a movie.

ROLLIN' JOE: I worked in a fitters in Govan, and a mate of mine there had a ticket for Jerry Lee Lewis. When Lewis cancelled he gave the ticket to me, so I went along to take a look. The Treniers headlined instead – and they blew me away! I remember walking down Renfield Street with the twin brothers, Claude and Cliff, completely caught up with the music they'd just played. And that was me a rock'n'roll fan!

I made it on my first night
Joe Moretti leads the charge into the big wide world

EARLY SCOTS stars Lonnie Donegan and Chas McDevitt had lived down south from an early age, so as yet there was no one who'd made it out of Scotland. And as the skiffle movement began to transform into something completely different, the way to the top was the road to the south. What's more, everyone knew where they were headed: straight to the 2 I's Coffee Bar.

JOE MORETTI: I was eighteen. I knew about the 2 I's, but there I was, first time in London, standing outside it... the place where Cliff Rochard and Tommy Steele had been discovered.

I asked Tom Littlewrood, the guy on the door, if I could play that night, and he said I could. It was my chance to earn a few quid – but only if I was good. There were no rules except you did it live; and if you couldn't cut it, you got off the stage. There were dozens of boys every night waiting to take your place.

So I just went for it: cranked the volume up and just played for about forty-five minutes or so. Just good, honest rock'n'roll. Then it sank in... people were enjoying it! Maybe I could make it in London after all! As soon as I came off I got offered a tour with Colin Hicks, Tommy Steele's brother – and I even got a few bucks up front.

I'd made it on my first night!

Tell Laura she's banned

Kids weren't ready for tear-jerker song, bosses believed

THE RELEASE of Ray Peterson's *Tell Laura I Love Her* was postponed because Decca Records bosses felt the kids wouldn't be able to handle the tear-jerking nature of the lyrics. Boy meets girl, boy wants to marry girl, boy meets financial problem over buying ring, boy meets stock car race with cash prize, boy meets technical issue with stock car, boy meets Grim Reaper, boy doesn't want to marry Grim Reaper, Grim Reaper has other ideas, girl cries alone in church as boy's dying words echo to fade.

Three months later, Ricky Valence's version of the song, released by Columbia, made it to number one for three weeks without any problems. Decca bosses had five board meetings about their future attitudes.

ELAINE MORTON: Ooh, it was so romantic! The *Jackie* magazine wasn't out, I don't think, but all that stuff was right up our street – photos of the pop stars you were going to marry and all that. I loved Adam Faith. I didn't know if he had a girlfriend but when our eyes met he'd *know* as well as I did, and that would be that! I remember looking through my mum's cook books, trying to work out the kind of cakes Adam might like me to bake for him... But *Tell Laura I Love Her* – Imagine having someone ready to die for you! Of course we cried about it, but we were all crying about different singers. At least, my friends better not have been thinking about Adam.

Not all it's cracked up to be

Realities of life on the road begin to hit home

GENE VINCENT was not enjoying life in the UK by 1960. After collapsing backstage at a Scottish gig, he survived the car crash in which Eddie Cochran was killed. He announced his daughter had died and he had to go home – but then a week later his manager admitted it had been a hoax to get him out of the country. In a press interview he'd said he felt inferior to British acts: 'They know all kinds of music, they discuss keys, arrangements and so on. They try to achieve perfection. I just sing – that's all I know.'

JOE MORETTI: Gene was a genuine superstar; no other word covers it. But in the short time I knew him, the person, he always seemed to be hurting inside. Loneliness was part of the bag in those days. The lifestyle fed the ego, but you had nowhere to hang your hat. Forget all the movies, the magazines and TV shows and the black leather – he just wanted to be one of the guys, and when I was in his band and he was hanging with us, that's who he was.

There was a night in Glasgow where the Empire just became a riot. The audience just wanted Gene. and when Billy Fury went on they started tearing the brass ash-trays off the seats and throwing them at the stage, shouting for Gene. In the end there were police everywhere. We didn't go on that night.

But I knew Gene was hankering for some good old southern-fried chicken and corn on the cob. I also knew you could get the best in Britain at Allan's Hotel in Kelvinside. Gene didn't believe me but we went along, and the manager did us proud. He gave us a private dining room and looked after every bit of detail – proper Scottish hospitality.

As the backing band we were always skint; we never even had the money to phone home to check everything was okay, but Gene would just put it on his expenses. And that was for all twelve of us!

He didn't know about 'fag' being a British word for cigarette – he just knew the American meaning: homosexual. So every time we talked about wanting a fag he'd say, 'Don't look at me baby… you got the wrong guy!' I had a lot of genuine affection for him, and I was no special case. God bless your memory, Gene.

PETER KERR, Clyde Valley Stompers: Travelling was murder. There was only one motorway, the M1, which went from the outskirts of London to Rugby. Everything else was single-lane trunk roads, so you'd spend hours and hours on end sitting behind streams of trucks. And you'd be doing runs like London to Birmingham and back again on the same night. Complete hell.

Jive Dive...
Complex dance checks out

CHUBBY CHECKER is proud to take credit for having introduced 'dancing apart to the beat' in 1960 – but it marked the end of one of the greatest traditions of original rock'n'roll.

ROLLIN' JOE: There were incredible jive clubs all over Glasgow. You paid your money and they taught you to jive. Glasgow jive was unique as well – we had a lot more moves, a lot more soul. It's important to realise rock'n'roll was a dance culture; it was about a band playing and people dancing. It wasn't really around for long. It was only around 1960 that ballrooms started taking on the Sabres, the Chaperones, the Redhawks from Dunfermline, and one or two others. Before that it was traditional dance bands who might play a bit of rock'n'roll for the jivers.

It was all about real dancing – and you didn't do it on your own either. If you tried, the men in white coats would come!

But the twist killed it stone dead. That bastard Chubby Checker came along and just killed rock'n'roll. After that there were all those other cheap dances from America – and every single one of them was shite. It had been a social event: the band learned to play, you learned to dance and everyone had a night out. Then it was gone.

I remember Sol Byron at the Hamilton Town Hall – that was the first time I saw people just standing around watching a wee band. You went to see Chuck Berry, Jerry Lee Lewis, all the greats, and of course you watched them; they were unique. So were the Stones, the Beatles, the Kinks and Alex Harvey. But just watching any old band?

Within a year jive was dead, and so was real rock'n'roll. Bill Haley came to the Barrowland. Bill Haley! I nipped out of work to try to buy tickets, thinking there'd be a big queue. Nothing. Same with the show – you could wander straight in no problem. The room was about quarter full, and only about half a dozen people were jiving. You can say what you like about Bill Haley, but he was rock'n'roll. Seeing him playing to an empty room… well, you knew it was over. Chubby Checker has a lot to answer for.

Don't give up the day job
Full-time work remains hard to come by

AS THE 1960s marched on ballrooms began, slowly and grudgingly at first, to give way to pop groups. More and more people wanted to hear them while fewer and fewer wanted to listen to jazz. Plus the pop groups were smaller, meaning venues could pay them less. Beat clubs began to open all over Scotland; whether they were beatnik bars, cool cafes or bohemian hangouts, they were all fuelling the fire.

PETE AGNEW, Nazareth: There hadn't really been much of a music scene for us – all the dance halls still had the big bands. You'd hardly ever see a group in there, and even if you could we were too young to get in! By now you were seeing groups a lot more often, although they were only special guests and the big bands played most of the night.

Then the clubs started up. At home we had the St.Margaret's Hall, which later burned down, and they had the Vandals in residency. The Cowdenbeath Palais, which *should* have burned down, had the Hellcats, and the Kinema Ballroom had The Redhawks. We wound up in the Kinema ourselves, much later on.

But no Scottish band ever really thought they'd end up making records. It just didn't happen. You did want to be a force to be reckoned with in Scotland, though. I think we achieved that – and the whole time, we never gave a thought to ever being a full-time band. Even the best-known bands on the circuit had day jobs.

ALAN MAIR, The Beatstalkers: Our singer, Davie Lennox, and I, both worked at Dalglish's as sheet metal draughtsmen. We'd been going for over a year by this point and we were doing really well wherever we went. We'd end up sleeping in the factory sometimes – if you were coming back from a gig in Aberdeen at five in the morning it made more sense to go straight to the factory than to try going home first.

All the bosses took us in – *all* the bosses, the MD and everyone, and we stood there with our heads bowed as they shook their fingers saying, 'It's not good enough. We know you're sleeping here. If it doesn't stop we'll have to let you go.'

We told them we were going to turn pro, but it just sounded like a big joke to them. No one realised what a following we had all over Scotland.

Four young lads from Liverpool
Bringing the beat boom

THE BEATLES completed their 1962-63 Hogmanay show in Hamburg then flew to London to start a Scottish tour. But with the weather against them the show scheduled for 2 January was abandoned; meaning their first appointment in the north of the nation – asides from having backed Johnny Gentle in 1960, with a guest drummer because they didn't have one yet – was on 3 January, at the Two Red Shoes in Elgin. They also played Dingwall Town Hall, the Museum Hall, Bridge of Allan, and the Beach Ballroom, Aberdeen, all for three shillings a ticket. But they left was a mixed impression.

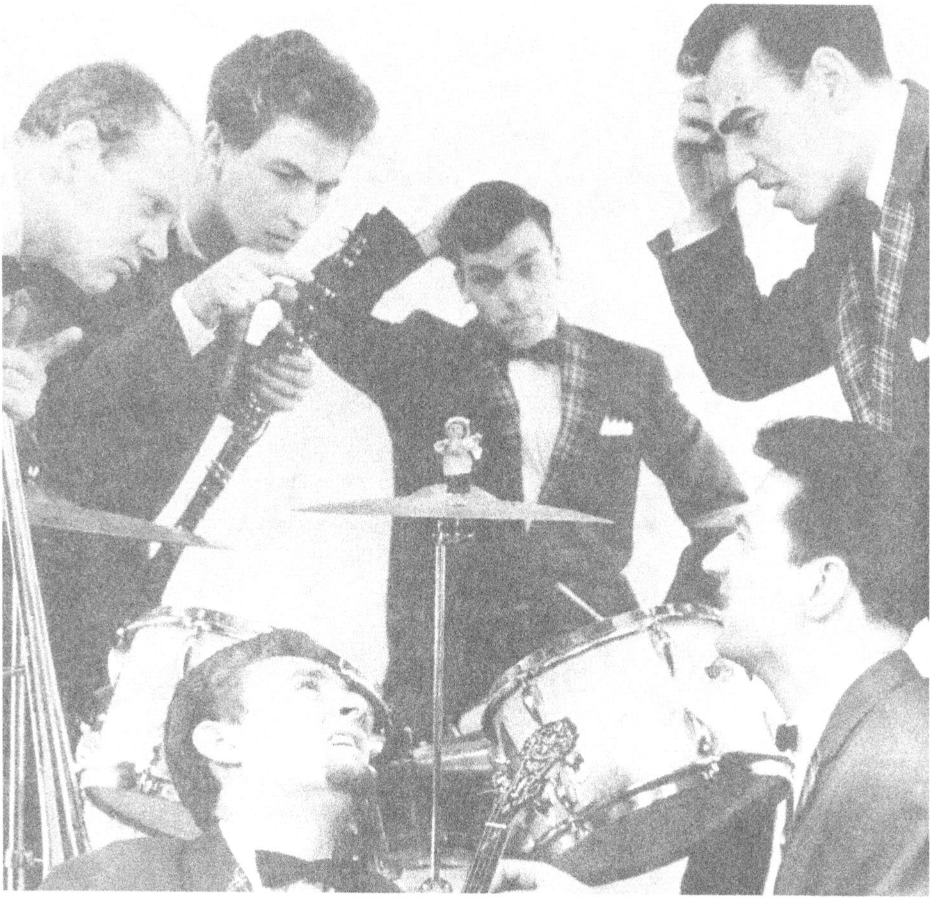

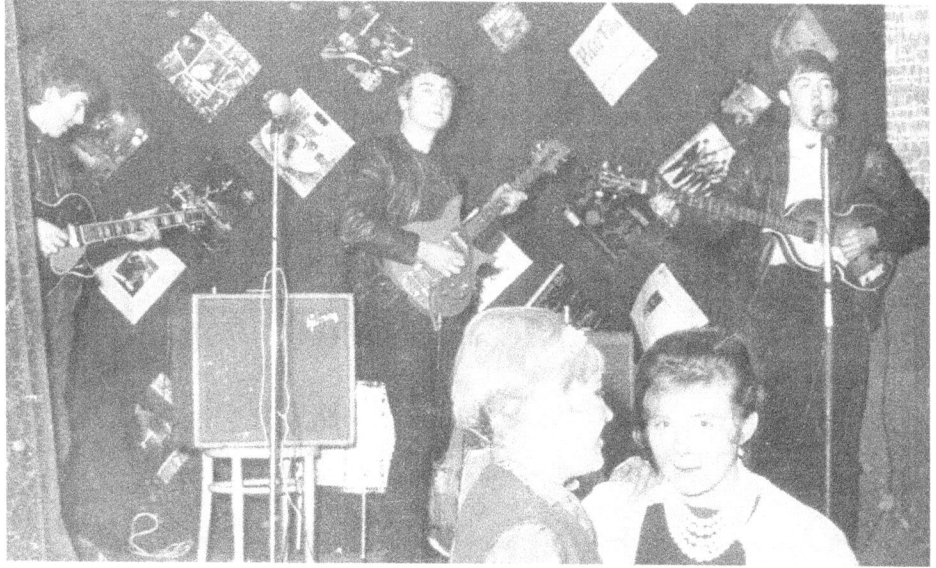

Above: the Clyde Valley Stompers   **Below: the Beatles in a small Scottish club early in their career**

COLIN MacINTOSH: You can always tell a good band, and without doubt they were that – but they didn't grab me. My girlfriend loved it; I'd seen better. If you ask me, Alex Harvey wiped the floor with the Beatles. I'd seen him a few months earlier and I found myself comparing everything to his show.

But when they dropped the covers and did one of their own tunes, you could feel things changing. They definitely had something there. Anyway, I was heading towards R&B. When I heard the Stones I knew I was right. The girlfriend didn't last either!

ANDY LOW: I thought the Beatles were incredible. The look, the delivery, the harmonies – it was a breath of fresh air. I'd seen so many copycat groups at the Beach Ballroom in Aberdeen, I really thought about giving up going to concerts; although God knows what else there was to do at the time.

But the Beatles brought it back to life. I thought, 'Hey, maybe I can do that,' and I borrowed my mate's guitar – then bought one myself. It's been a big part of my life ever since. I never joined a band and never went on stage; and I never really wanted to. But it's still important to me.

ROB MITCHELL: People were screaming right the way through the songs. I thought, 'This is a great way to get girls!' Although to be fair, they more or less did that at every gig. The other thing was, you didn't have to learn the words because of all the screaming – you just needed to know the chorus!

The Fab Four had been advertised as 'The Love Me Do Boys,' such was the doubt over whether they'd sell tickets. But as they rocketed towards stardom they signalled the end of a number of eras – not least for the dying embers of the trad jazz world.

FIONNA DUNCAN, Clyde Valley Stompers: All the gigs we played up and down the country, unless they were in trad-jazz clubs, were two-band sessions. We topped the bill, and the support act, then known as the interval group, was usually the big local band to bring in more kids – or an accordion and fiddle group to cater for the older members of the audience who actually thought we were too loud!

I vividly remember playing one time at the Cavern Club in Liverpool. We arrived early to set up and there was already a massive queue at the entrance. We wondered if our new album had snuck into the hit parade without our noticing.

But it wasn't that; it was the interval group, four young boys in black. I remember giggling when I heard they were calling themselves 'The Beatles.'

PETER KERR, Clyde Valley Stompers: If we had a blank in the datesheet on a Sunday, our agency would put us in the Cavern. What a shithole place that was to play. I don't think it would be allowed now. It was just a tunnel, and it got jam-packed, you couldn't breathe, you couldn't move and you were soaked in sweat on a tiny wee stand, and the dressing room was a cupboard. The acoustics were dreadful too. But the atmosphere was electric among the punters, because they were right there in it. It was like one big punter – you didn't really have much choice!

But it was always a jazz club, and all those Liverpool bands that came out later had been our interval acts. Being jazz men – you know we can be a bit snobby – we thought they were all crap. Because the scene was in transition you'd find a lot of those early beat groups were made to record trad songs, stuff from the 1920s and such. The record labels weren't sure what was happening next so they'd play it safe and have the beat tracks and some jazz tracks too. I don't think many of those groups would have wanted to be playing those songs...

The Great Train Wrongery

Police overestimate power of a band's second-hand van

PETE AGNEW, Nazareth**:** As the Shadettes we used to play Burntisland Palais every Saturday night. Sometimes we'd play the local cinema afterwards during the midnight horror presentations – movies with names like *The Wasp Woman*...

We had a knackered ex-gas board van, painted bright yellow, and we wore bright yellow suits with a black 'S' embroidered on the pocket. To our eternal shame, now! When we finished at about 4am we'd be too tired to bother changing clothes, so we'd just pack up and head home.

One time like that, it was the morning of 9 August 1963, and just after we chugged up the hill out of Burntisland we were pulled over by a police car. Two cops told us to get out of the van and unload it. We asked what the problem was, and they said there'd been a train robbery and a lot of money was involved.

They said it had happened a couple of hours earlier, and we thought it must have been at Aberdour or Kirkaldy or somewhere like that. But they said it was in Buckinghamshire – four hundred miles away! And we're in a bright yellow van in bright yellow suits, mind you!

We were probably the first, and definitely the most colourful, suspects in the Great Train Robbery...

An apology to Katie Girvan

...but nursing school had nothing on joining a band

EDDIE JOHNSON, Hi Fi Combo: The band was formed by two brothers from Kilbirnie, Dick and Andy Sneddon. Dick was the drummer and Andy played bass. They recruited Glaswegian Kenny Munro on guitar, and a singer with an amazing range, Tommy Gray, from Lochwinnoch.

They reckoned music on the Tamla Motown label would be the next big thing, at a time when most bands were playing chart covers. They began to search for the perfect organist to complete the line-up – and that's where I came in.

I was starting my second-year exams at Ballochmyle Hospital when they turned up at my dormitory room. They knew I'd been playing piano in my own band and asked me to play something for them.

I took them to the recreation hall where there was a grand piano, and played the *Theme from Exodus*, plus a piece by Mozart. Then Dick asked in his strange brogue, 'Dae ye wahnt tae jine oor bonn? Wi'v bin searchin' furra perfect organist – but ye'll huv ti' dae...'

As they frightened me terribly, I declined their offer, but they offered me stardom in both Germany and Britain, a record deal and millions of pounds, which I felt was pretty generous considering they all looked poverty-stricken.It seemed a little better than the £2 a week I'd earn with my Registered General Nurse Certificate. I resigned from the hospital and bade farewell to my nursing girlfriend Katie Girvan. Katie, wherever you are, I'm sorry about that scribbled note I put under your door...

A girl just like me

If it's good enough for Lulu...

LULU and the Luvvers made number seven in mid-64 with their cover of the Isley Brothers' track *Shout!* starring fifteen-year-old Marie Lawrie's middle-aged vocal. Inspired when she'd heard Alex Harvey singing the number, she'd teamed up with a band called Gleneagles and they'd become the near-enough overnight sensation breakthrough act Scotland so badly needed. They appeared on *Top of the Pops* on 3 and 10 June, surrounded by Brian Poole and the Tremeloes, the Dave Clark Five and the Swinging Blue Jeans – and did it all without the aid of tartan.

ANNE BROWN: A girl my age on *Top of the Pops*? From my home town? Now you're talking! Watching the show was about the only time me and my big brother agreed on anything. I told him right there, 'I'm joining your group!' And since they didn't have a singer he let me.

All I could do at first was Lulu's 'Weeell...' bit. Still, it was a start. Soon I was getting into the Stones and a whole world of music. But then my parents cut in – they wanted me to be a good little girl and not a rocker, and there was certainly no way I was going on stage. My brother stood up for me, but no one could talk them round, and that was that. I still do *Shout!* at the karaokes and family parties, but my brother gave up the guitar in the 60s. Parents! And I should know – I'm one now...

Beat riot
An unexpected turnout

WITH THE GAYLORDS having headed to London to seek their fortune and become Marmalade on the way, the jury was split between the Pathfinders and the Beatstalkers as to who was the biggest band in Scotland. Let there be no doubt: big meant big. Witness the proceedings in Glasgow's George Square, when the Beatstalkers decided to put on a free show for a couple of hundred fans.

ALAN MAIR, The Beatstalkers: That was the wildest and most bizarre thing ever. My mum said I should put an advert in the *Sunday Mail*, but I said it wouldn't be right, and there'd be a few hundred people there anyway. The day came and we were sitting in the manager's office, a few hundred yards from the square, and one of the roadies phoned: 'There's hundreds... there's *thousands* of people here!' We knew the Tongs, one of the hardest gangs in Glasgow, and we asked them to get a few people there because there were only two policemen. But when we arrived we still had to fight our way to the stage!

We got to play one number – but people were rushing the stage, pushing in every direction, and the Tongs were shouting, 'We can't hold them back!' The two police had gone to their TARDIS and phoned for more police, and there was a press helicopter above us, and the mounted police galloped in, and I'm thinking, 'This is out of control!'

The police told us we'd need to stop playing, and that's when everyone went nuts. They must have been thinking, 'I want a piece of them before they go!' The stage started coming forward and the police told us to get out over the back and get into

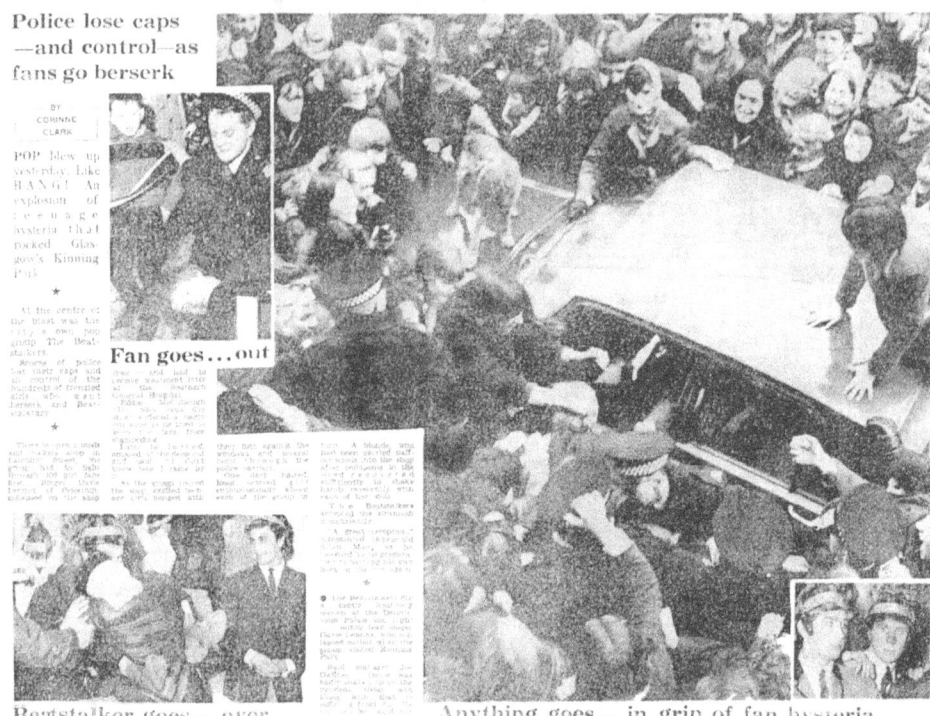

BEATSTALKRAZY!

Police lose caps —and control—as fans go berserk

BY
CORINNE
CLARK

POP blew up yesterday. Like BANG! An explosion of teenage hysteria that rocked Glasgow's Kinning Park.

★

At the centre of the blast was the city's own pop group The Beatstalkers.

Scores of police lost their caps and all control of the hundreds of frenzied girls who want Beatles and Beatstalkers.

★

Fan goes...out

Beatstalker goes...over

Anything goes...in grip of fan hysteria

Above: coverage of the Beatstalker riot in Glasgow's George Square
Below: the Hi Fi Combo – Dick and Andy Sneddon, Kenny Murno, Tommy Gray and Eddie Johnstone

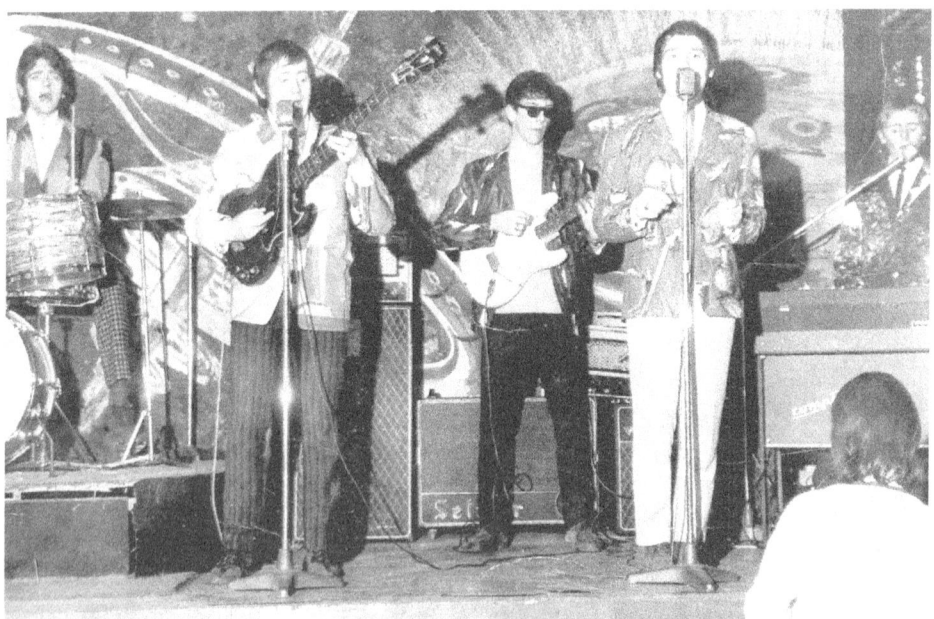

the City Chambers. Tudge and Ronnie ended up on the back of police horses – tally ho! We were very bedraggled by the time we made the 80 yards in to the Chambers. It was national news... all the papers covered it, front page and everything!

I got home before my mum finished work, and she said, 'How did it go?' I said, 'Aye, okay...' She said, 'You should have put it in the *Sunday Mail* – it would probably have gone better.' I said, 'Maybe. Have you seen the paper?'

We were doing very well by then – we'd gone pro the year before, despite what our bosses had said. We'd bought a *Z Cars* car, the Zephyr 4. I used to never understand why people were staring at me, but I was seventeen, looked twelve, and I'm driving this really flashy car! We knew all the bosses at the factory sat with the guys at lunchtime, so Davie and I drove up in the Zephyr 4 at just the right time. We didn't have to say anything; our faces told the story: ,'See, we knew!'

We could go into McCormack's to buy expensive music gear with cash, and we'd take even more cash in so we could wave it about and show off. There were girls sleeping outside all our flats... I remember crawling across the floor from the bedroom to the kitchen, so they wouldn't see me through the front door window, just so I could have an hour to myself before the doorbell started ringing. One night there were twenty-five girls in the close. We were recognised by grannies, young kids – it was mind-blowing! And the great thing is, it saw us through those problematic puberty years, when you don't really know what to do with yourself.

Rock them off the beaches
Pirate radio weighs anchor

THE MID-ATLANTIC accent came about when pirate DJs wanted to distance themselves from the stuffy kind of delivery you'd normally expect on UK radio. The style was a statement: we're a bit exotic; we want to be part of the rock'n'roll dream; we share your aspirations; we're like you. And we're most certainly not like *them*.

It began with Radio Caroline and there were others, but north of the border, and across much of England and Ireland, the happening sounds were broadcast from the mast of the *Comet*, a converted Clyde-built lightship from 1904. The plan was for a big party launch in the tradition of a Scottish Hogmanay, but after a trial of technical trickery the station managed to get up and running on 242 metres just minutes before 1966.

Radio Scotland is playing just for you
So beat the ban and join the clan
On station 242!

By broadcasting from international waters pirate stations were able to loop a loophole in the law, and thus play songs about people dying in car crashes if they bloody well wanted to. With its magazine, its Clan Fan Club and regular Clan Balls all over the country, Radio Scotland was the big noise on the music scene.

JOHN KERR, DJ: I remember many pop stars coming out to visit when they were playing Scotland – Cat Stevens and Gene Pitney were regulars. Once I got fairly excited about an upcoming visit from an Australian star, Normie Rowe. I'd compered a lot of his shows so I'd been bragging to all the DJs about this tall, good-looking guy – I knew what a star he was, especially with the girls. Normie arrived out on the *Comet's* tender on a pretty rough-sea day, stepped onboard and promptly threw up on the deck. So much for the macho star I'd been portraying...

MEL HOWARD, DJ: I'll never forget one of those pirate picture-perfect early evenings. It was a warm summer day with no wind to speak of, and the *Comet* was sitting quietly on a glass sheet. It was bliss. The crew had finished dinner and had gone below to rest, read or tend to chores. I'd just started a taped programme that featured Garner Ted Armstrong bringing us The World Tomorrow – thirty minutes of modern religion, delivered like only GTA could.

I was sitting out over the bow, daydreaming, when I became aware of a low rumbling sound that seemed to be coming from the depths just a few yards away from me. I noticed a series of bubbles and ripples forming on the surface... then the bubbling became boiling. I'd never witnessed anything like it – it was like an undersea volcano was about to erupt right in front of me!

Then, up from this cauldron of seething water emerged a submarine! I'd only ever seen one in books, and now there it was dwarfing our little vessel. I was silently rooted to the spot. I hadn't taken my eyes off the scene, nor had I called any of the crew to join me. Then a figure appeared in a rubber suit, climbed out of the sub's tower, launched a dinghy, and began heading towards the *Comet*.

Back at the office, there was one absolute rule that had to be obeyed. Given the controversy that swirled around the presence of the pirates and the political beach ball it had become, our boss, Tommy Shields, demanded that, if we were challenged by any representative of Her Majesty's Government at sea, we were immediately to cease transmission. So I ran aft, calling our captain, Willie Fisher, and shouting, 'All hands on deck!' It was showdown time.

The naval officer asked for permission to come aboard and the skipper granted it. At that precise moment, Garner Ted Armstrong was silenced. We were off the air. The officer was up on our deck in an instant... I fought the urge to raise my hands. Surely I wasn't going to be arrested? That would be silly, wouldn't it?

Finally he told us, 'We've been doing manoeuvres in this area. One of our exercises was to set foot on a place that wasn't a part of our vessel. So we chose you!'

All thoughts of arrest vanished, a bottle of the ship's best rum soon materialised and Willie the skipper poured tots. Everyone had a laugh when our side of the story was told – and we were delighted to learn that Radio Scotland was often heard in the crew's quarters when the sub was in the area. What could be sweeter? The bottle was emptied and our new shipmate waved his goodbyes. Garner Ted Armstrong returned to the air and Radio Scotland was back in business, doing what it did best: bringing the beat of the 60s to those above and below the waves.

Just like not being there
Absent band keeps 2000 fans mesmerised

EDDIE TOBIN, manager and agent: The Bo-Weavles, the band I looked after, were huge. But they weren't as big as the Beatstalkers. We had to actually be at a show and perform before the audience were satisfied. The Beatstalkers didn't. We opened for them at the Dennistoun Palais – and they weren't even there. After the Weavles had played the big rotating stage turned round to reveal cardboard cutouts of the Beatstalkers, and a phone on a table.

The phone rang and the sold-out room went quiet. There were 2000 people there, even though it had been billed as 'Not the Beatstalkers,' as a guy picked up the phone, said, 'Hello?' then told them: 'It's Davie Lennox, singer from the Beatstalkers!' They went crazy! But they weren't there.

They weren't there as much as a big velvet curtain wasn't there after the Weavles played the Queens Halls in Dunoon. The curtain was never seen again – but the band had lovely new velvet suits to wear on stage.

Street fighting men
All part of the night's entertainment for some people

A VERY WISE old editor once told me the best journalists were people who would be in jail if they hadn't found newspapers. Perhaps that same is true of musicians, certainly from the first quarter century of Scottish rock'n'roll. Everyone viewed nights out at concerts as an escape from working-class drudgery. For the musicians there was at least half a spitting chance of it being permanent. But in early 1968, for many of the lads and lassies who went home to the schemes of Scotland once the house lights came up, it was a different story. Some spoke with six strings wired into an amp... others spoke with five fingers wrapped into a fist.

MARTIN GRIFFITHS, Beggars Opera: First time we experienced any of that was while we were taking group photos in Rouken Glen Park, and we came across a guy who'd been attacked with an open razor. When we started to play at youth clubs and school halls there would always be a gang presence. Their girls would take sharpened steel combs into the dance and we'd end up hanging on to our equipment while chairs and kids flew through the air.

I remember at one dance at Stamperland, south of Glasgow, being approached by three members of a well-known gang and 'asked' to play *Satisfaction* by the Stones. It was lucky we knew it because, later on, the same guys threw acid at a couple walking near Clarkston Toll.

For veteran crooner Frankie Vaughan, the crowd behaviour at his Glasgow Pavillion show was enough to make him want to go down there and sort it out. 'Down there', in this case, was Easterhouse, and since Frankie was already heavily involved in boys' clubs (they'd sorted him out when he was a wean himself) he decided to spearhead a weapons amnesty.

Papers dripped with the story, and photo opportunities abounded. There's still a lot of goodwill to his memory – he died in 1999 – but, according to some of the kids involved, there was really very little substance to the whole event.

RAB S: I can't even mind who it was, but somebody or other had started it up at Frankie's concert – it might have been the Paks. After that we heard he wanted everyone to hand in their knives. He said if we did, he'd build a community centre. We didn't care about it much, but when Frankie came to the estate we were all there to see it.

Suddenly you had TV people handing you a knife and a couple of bob, and telling us, 'Drop the knife in the bin there...' I went back four or five times. One time a guy asked the cameraman what he was doing, and he said, 'This kid's already handed the knife in – I'm just getting the shot of it.'

But he'd given it to me, out a van they'd brought. They were more tooled up than any of us!

MICK SLAVEN: You could tell Frankie Vaughan's heart was in the right place. I think he'd had a hard time when he was young, so he wanted everyone to learn from him. But nobody was really caring. Even the police didn't believe it was really happening. It didn't really change anything for us.

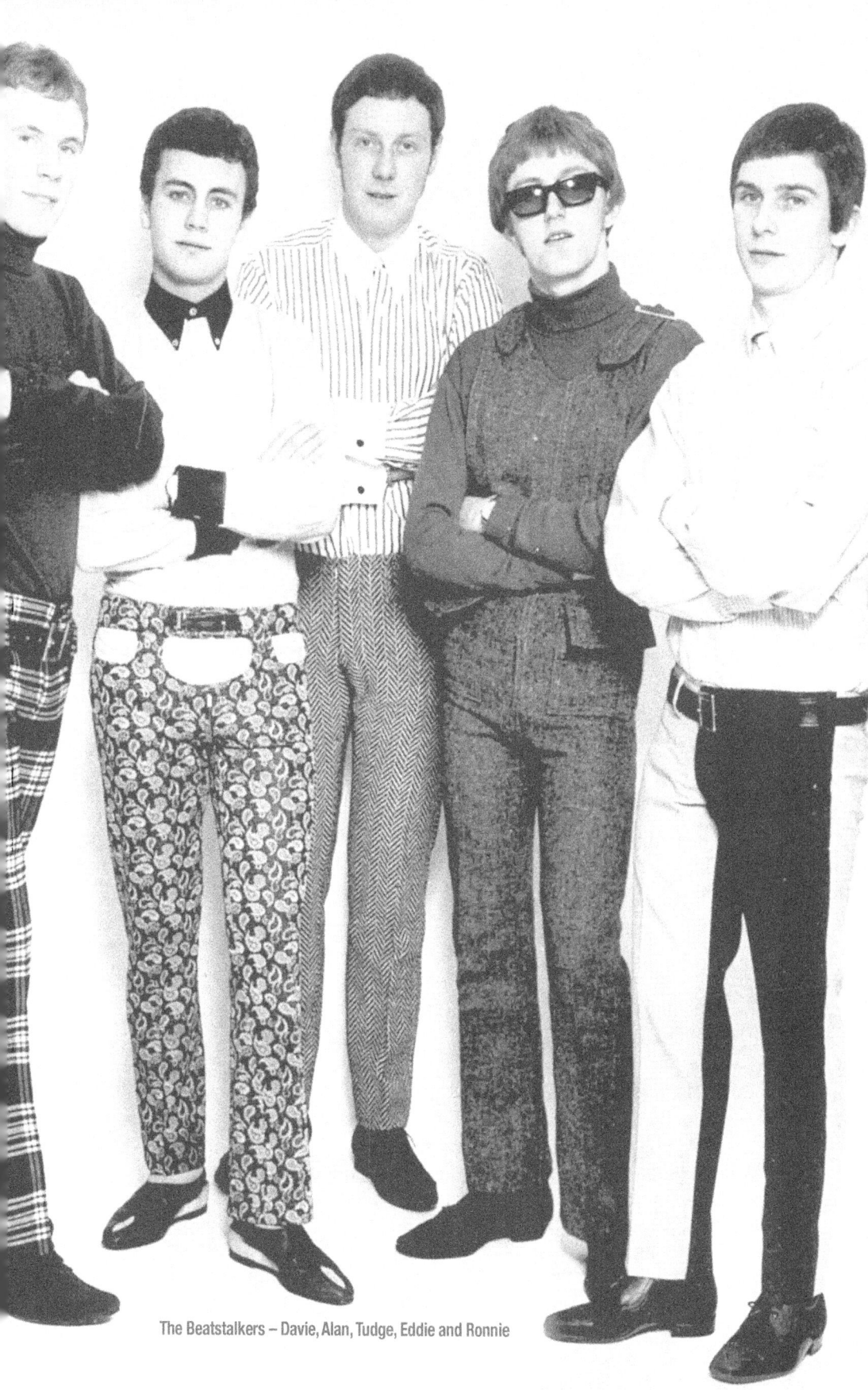

The Beatstalkers – Davie, Alan, Tudge, Eddie and Ronnie

A time to stop
Beatstalkers call it a day

THE BEATSTALKERS followed the traditional route to London and enjoyed a minor hit with *Silver Treetop School For Boys*, written for them by David Bowie. But when their van was stolen and they were faced with spending £4000 in 1960s money on a replacement vehicle and gear, it occurred to them that, perhaps, the situation represented a hint from above.

ALAN MAIR, The Beatstalkers: The live thing was carrying us on and people were still coming to see us, but it wasn't growing any more. We talked about replacing all the stuff we'd lost – there was no insurance, of course – and I just said, 'You know what, guys? I think it's time to call it a day.' So we did. I've always thought of these moments as the start of something new instead of the end of something old. It was time. And we recently discovered how it had been stolen... It was a trick that had been pulled on one or two other bands, so we'd suspected it but didn't know for sure. When the van went in for a service, people who worked there took a note of the registration, made spare keys and passed them on to someone else for a fee.

That only came up when we had the reunion show – for years some of us thought Ronnie had left the van open when he'd run into the Post Office. He hadn't known that! He was saying, 'What, all these years you thought it was me who'd ended the band?'

Sign the crows
Led Zep manager parks limo outside Glasgow pub

ROBERT LOW: I saw Stone the Crows being made at the Burns Howff... Maggie Bell, a bit of a wee stoatir then, and Les Harvey and the guys were in a nice wee group called Power. They played all the time at the Howff – I humped beer crates for nothing just to listen to the bands that gigged there.

But I'd never heard Maggie sing yet.

So this night a limo parked up. Nowadays you have stretch limos for daft wee twelve-year-old lassies having a birthday, but back then a limo in Glasgow was like seeing a two-headed cow coming down Sauchiehall Street. These guys all piled out, and they were English – and worse, they were Cockney wanker English... They swaggered in and listened to Maggie and the boys. Actually, they listened to the boys – it must have been the worst gig Power ever played, and they picked that night to do it. You couldn't hear Maggie's voice at all – so you know how loud the band must have been.

Still, the limo mob must have liked it; it turned out it was Peter Grant, the big fat beardie who managed Led Zeppelin. He signed them, and the rest, as they say, is history. I heard the new name, Stone the Crows, came from what he said when he first heard them, but I don't know if it's true. Les' guitar was cranked up so far you couldn't hear yourself breathe, never mind overhear any Cockney wankerisms.

Flash ahead to March 2006, the Renfrew Ferry and the British Blues Quintet. There I am, still ligging with a bus pass. So, to my surprise, is Maggie – she sang Free's *Wishing Well*, Leo Sayer's *My Life* and Etta James' *I Just Wanna Make Love to You*. Just three songs, and I wished it had been three times that. It took me nearly forty years, but I heard Maggie Bell sing live at last.

When Freddie met Bowie at a market stall
Star moment should have been photographed... but wasn't

In March 1974 Mariner 10 sent photos back from Mercury – but there was a totally different Mercury on everyone's mind: the Freddie one. Queen's *Seven Seas of Rhye* thundered into the top ten and announced the arrival of one of the UK's biggest and best musical exports. One ex-Beatstalker was very relieved.

ALAN MAIR: When the Beatstalkers finished we were all twenty-one or so, and even then you were thinking, rock'n'roll is a game for the kids. I had a wife and a son, a couple of the others guys were married... You really do think it's time to get a proper job.

I wound up running a stall in Kensington Market, making leather boots. It did very well – at one point everyone was wearing them. There's photos on album sleeves with the whole band wearing my boots! And I remember sitting in a wee cafe in Amsterdam, a wee place with a clothes workshop, and I overheard someone saying the zip had gone on one of his boots. I realised it was a pair of mine, so I said, 'I'm Alan Mair, give me the boot and I'll fix it for you!' I used the wee workshop in the cafe and it was no problem. It turned out the guy was the bass player from Golden Earring, so that was me hanging about with them...

I had Freddie Mercury working in the stall with me for a couple of years. He used to tell everyone he had a band going, and it wouldn't be long before he turned professional. A lot of the folks from the market went to see their first show – and they were terrible!

People remember Freddie for his moments like Live Aid – but back in the beginning he was a very awkward performer, and he had a tendency to sing sharp. I've always been very critical of live gigs anyway, but it was a bad show. He'd been telling everyone, 'I'm going professional soon, I won't be working with Alan for long...' and here was Queen, just not very good at all! The conversation at the pub afterwards was, how are we going to tell him? But in the end we just couldn't bring him down.

I really thought that was that, until one day I was listening to the radio in the van and thought, 'What a great song...' I couldn't believe it when the DJ said, 'That's a new band, Queen, with *Seven Seas of Rhye*.' I arrived at the market and told Freddie, 'That's it, you'll definitely be turning professional soon.'

Years later when they headlined the Rainbow I told him what I'd thought about that first show. He was shocked: 'Whaaat?'

'Yeah, it was pretty dire...'

'Oh well – I'm glad you didn't say then!'

The stall gave me the best camera moment of my life, although I didn't have a camera on me. I'd known David Bowie since the Beatstalkers did his song *Silver Tree Top School for Boys*. We used to go to gigs together. Just after *Space Oddity* was a hit he came to the stall, and I thought maybe he was looking for a pair of boots. 'No,' he said, 'I just came to say hello – I haven't got any money!'

'You haven't got any money? You've just had a hit record! Och, just have a pair – I'll treat you. Here, Freddie will fit them on for you.' What a photo that would have been!

Rollermania
The sudden rise of the tartan tearaways

WITHIN an eight-week period in 1974 the Bay City Rollers went from half-full clubs to sold-out halls, twenty-foot protective barriers, crowd crushes and helicopter escapes. It seems strange to relate the insanity to a reasonably sedate figure of just four top ten hits during 1974, although the album *Rollin'* got stuck in the charts for over a year; but it's a demonstration of how well all those events were manipulated by the band's management.

SUSAN CLEARMONT: I had *everything* – the singles, the stickers, the posters that said they were 'kissable size'. I fell out with my best friend because she fancied Woody too. Sorry, Helen, wherever you are! We all went to see them on their first big tour – we were still talking then – and on the night I noticed that, if you fainted, you got taken backstage. So I decided... I'm going to faint! I fought my way up to the first few rows and made sure one of the security men was watching, then just fell over. I was terrified – as soon as I was pretending to be unconscious, I had to keep my eyes closed, and I had to let the crowd drag me around. I nearly fainted for real!

Then I felt myself being lifted up and out, and I could tell I was over the barrier. I really wanted to open my eyes and try to get on the stage – Woody was only a few feet away from me by now – but I knew I'd be in trouble, so I kept on play-acting.

Next thing I knew I could feel fresh air. They weren't letting you backstage at all – they were taking you out of the hall! Soon I was standing in a small crowd of crying girls, who'd obviously all had the same idea. They let us back in at the back of the hall but there was no chance of getting near the group again. Asides from the kissable posters, that's the nearest I ever got to Woody...

STEVIE HUNTER: I thought the Rollers were great, but you couldn't really say that, could you? I saw Les McKeown when he was in Threshold and I thought he was good then, so I was into the Rollers before the girls were. Come on – what's wrong with *Bye Bye, Baby*? Perfect pop music, and it took them round the world, so you can't just write them off.

MARIE BRYSON: People talk about the Rollers all the time, but they forget Slik – they were all the rage too back at the start. I remember seeing both of them on the same night. That was a young Scots girl's dream come true. And Midge Ure looks better than Les these days...

DAVID PATON, Pilot: I didn't leave the Rollers on the brink of success without thinking it through. I came to realise I didn't want to be a Roller – no matter how successful they'd become. There was no Les, Woody or Eric in the band when I'd been there, but I still saw the way it was going. I didn't want any part of it. I did find Rollermania quite amusing, though! I got on well with Alan and Derek and they were always very confident it was going to happen for them. When it did, I knew how happy they were and how much dedication it had taken.

The Rollers would never have been a long-term commitment for me. I saw it as part of my apprenticeship. Tam Paton, their manager – no relation! – had his dream and he was definitely pulling the strings. It wasn't my dream... I achieved that with Pilot. Writing a worldwide number one is surely the goal of every composer.

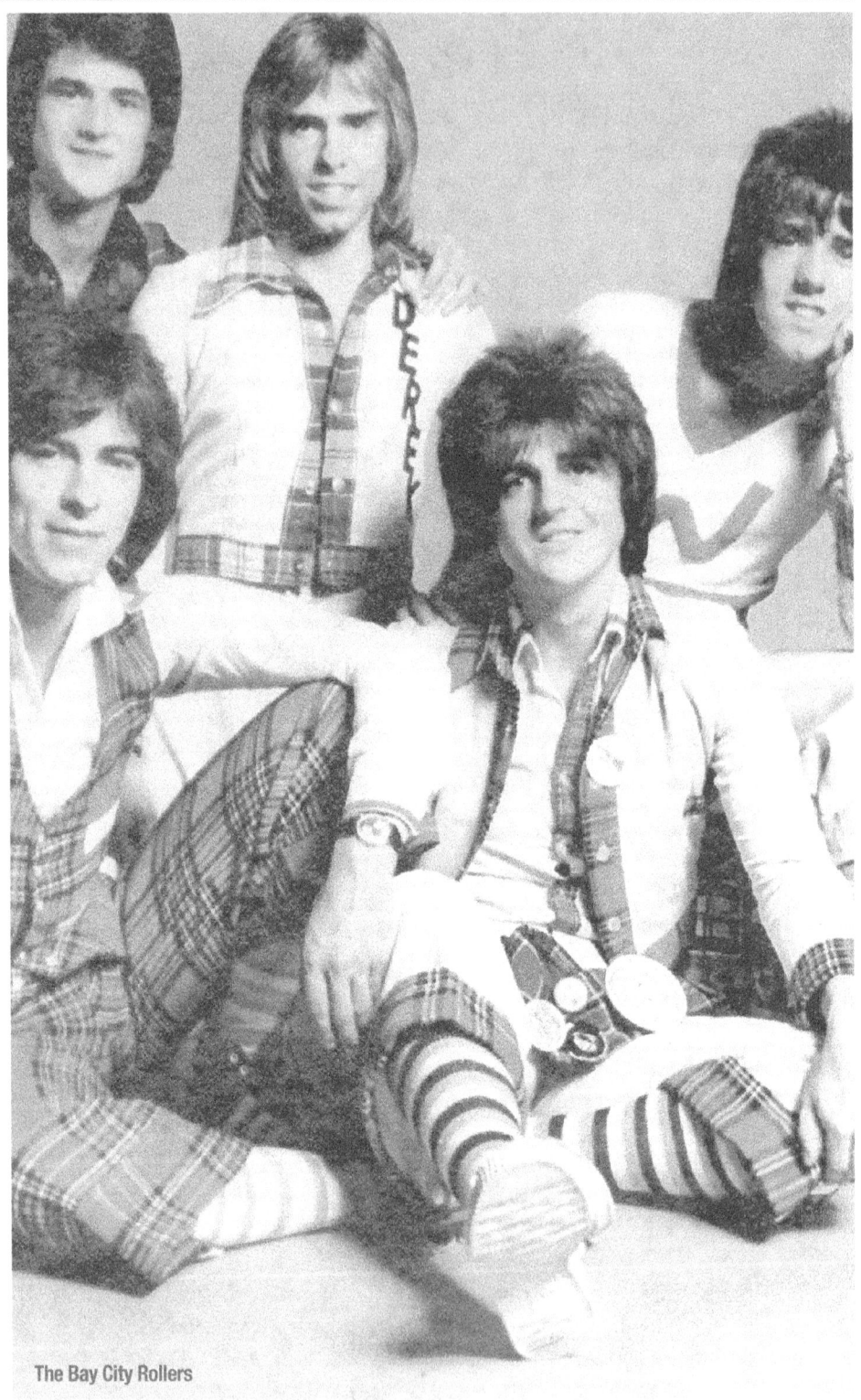

The Bay City Rollers

The Rollers had always made a point of avoiding the heavier and harder Glasgow circuit, correctly viewing it as incompatible with their pop aims. That's not and never to say they couldn't have done the do amid the long-haired rockers, no matter how challenging it might have been. But the long-hairs were having their own problems, because Glasgow promoters were trying to shunt them in the direction of Les and the lads.

BRIAN YOUNG, CaVa Studios: Northwind's album sold twenty thousand copies in 1972, but due to the usual poor management control we made nothing financially. We'd gained a lot musically, though, and we had some great support gigs including Yes, Free, and Fleetwood Mac at the Green's Playhouse before it became the Apollo. We headlined a concert at Wolverhampton Civic Hall when Deep Purple couldn't make it. But the fun came to an end when Glasgow promoters started insisting that everyone should play disco. Some bands kept going, but only by giving up Scotland. Sad...

The mafia stole my guitar
SAHB's mixed fortunes

THE SENSATIONAL Alex Harvey Band were on the road in the USA in the mid-70s when two things happened: the mafia stole their guitars and a release they hadn't known about made the top ten, requiring them to belt home for *Top of the Pops*.

CHRIS GLEN, SAHB: We woke up and the truck was gone from outside the hotel – simple as that. Turned out it was a pretty standard trick with some family people, if you know what I mean. Then we got the telegram: 'Single's in the top ten, you need to come back quick.' Hold on... what single?

The whole story came out. We'd asked to have our show at the Hammersmith Odeon recorded because we had some new systems in and we wanted to have a listen. Our manager, Bill Fehilly, had heard the tape and said, 'Get that out there as an album, and get *Delilah* out as a single.'

They needed a hit – they'd tried everything including having people like Errol Brown writing songs for us. You should have heard that shite... 'A hungry man must eat, a tired man must sleep, but when I am in love I want to make love...'

But we knew there'd be a problem: as soon as you have one hit the label needs another one, and you're on a conveyor belt until you fall off, or you're pushed. We only ever did *Delilah* because we wanted something we could do a stupid dance to. The fans had loved the dance we did with *Runaway* and *Delilah* was meant to replace that. End of story. So they had fly back to the UK first class for once, which cost £1200 a ticket. I woke up on the plane, still pished, and opened my shutter to see this beautiful sunrise. Suddenly a trolley-dolly leaned over and shut it again, but I was like, 'For £1200 I'll have my sunrise, thank you!' She said, 'No, you can,'t, sir, the Indian Ambassador (or whoever) wants to sleep.' But he's paying the same as me! So in the end they let me have the run of the upstairs bar, just to get me out the way.

TED McKENNA, SAHB: I was recently talking to someone I'd known thirty years ago. She was saying, 'I couldn't remember why I didn't like your band, then I heard *Delilah* on the radio and I remembered – I don't like comedy bands.' So that was us, a comedy band. I don't think we ever shook that off with some people.

How I joined Thin Lizzy
Robbo's road to stardom started in hotel drinking session

PHIL Lynott's Thin Lizzy had been in the wars line-up-wise, but the band broke through at last, bringing with it the twin-guitar sound which was to inspire the new wave of British heavy metal a few years later on. And guess what? Like all the best tricks, it came about by accident, part-engineered by Scots six-stringer Brian 'Robbo' Robertson.

BRIAN ROBERTSON, Thin Lizzy: I joined the band soon after I'd been fired from a music shop for nicking records and guitar strings. The guy's wages were crap, so I'd thought, 'I'll just pay myself!'

I met Lizzy when they were a three-piece, although I didn't meet Eric Bell that time. They were staying at a hotel just down the road from my house. My best mate, Big Charlie, was roadying for them, so I went into the hotel bar after I finished a gig. I ended up sitting down with Phil and Brian Downey and we had a lot to drink. I went to Downey's room and we went through lots of blues stuff – he was hitting the bed with sticks and I was playing my guitar without an amp.

When Eric Bell left they started holding auditions, and Charlie said, 'Remember that mate of mine from Glasgow?' So I got a train down to London and ended up staying in a squat with the roadies for about a month. I got the last audition – Phil was going to call it a day. Downey remembered me straight away from the night in the hotel, and we just took it from there.

I think Phil wanted to keep it a three-piece but Downey and I wanted another guitarist. Being honest, I don't think I was good enough to carry it as a three-piece!

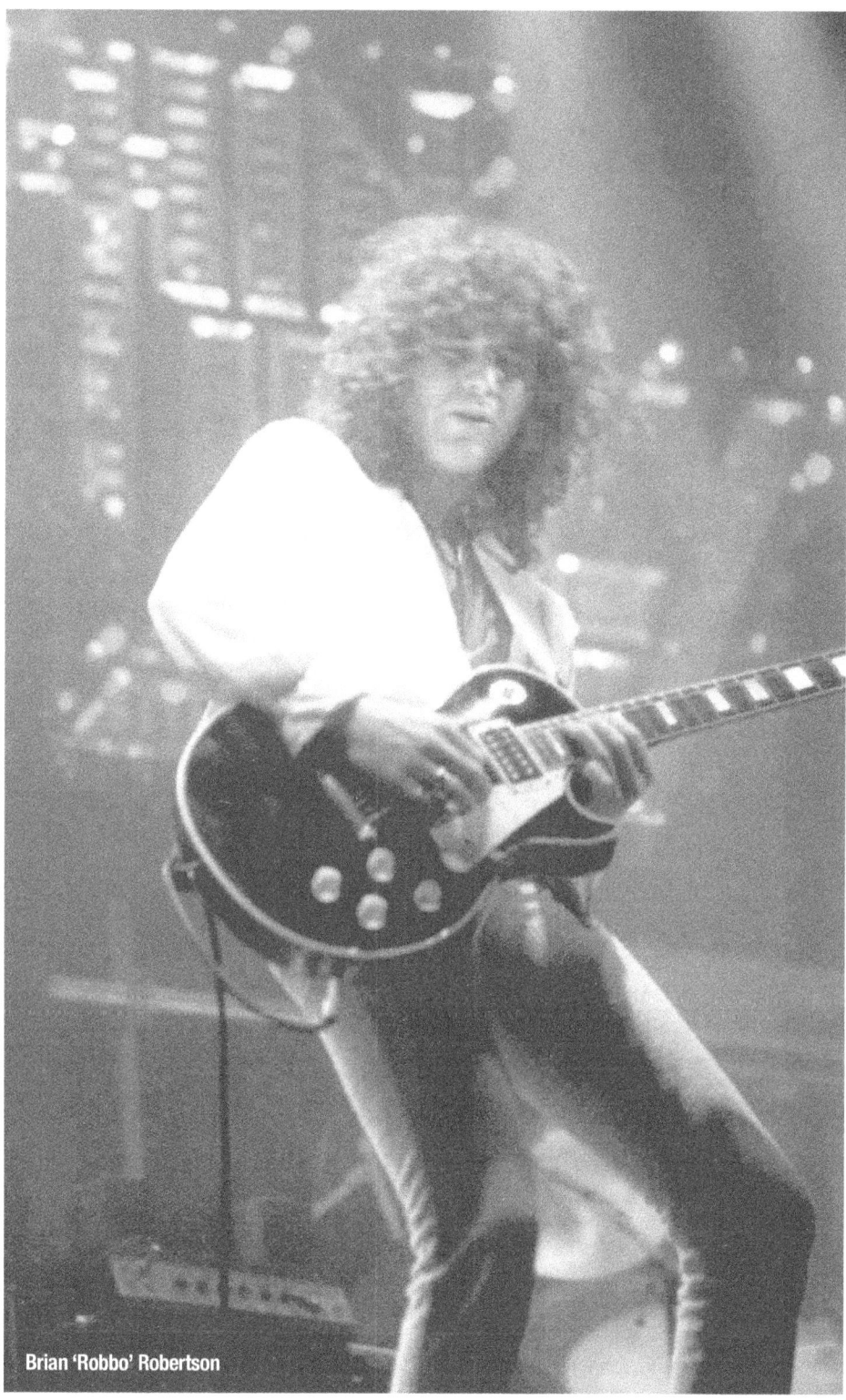

Brian 'Robbo' Robertson

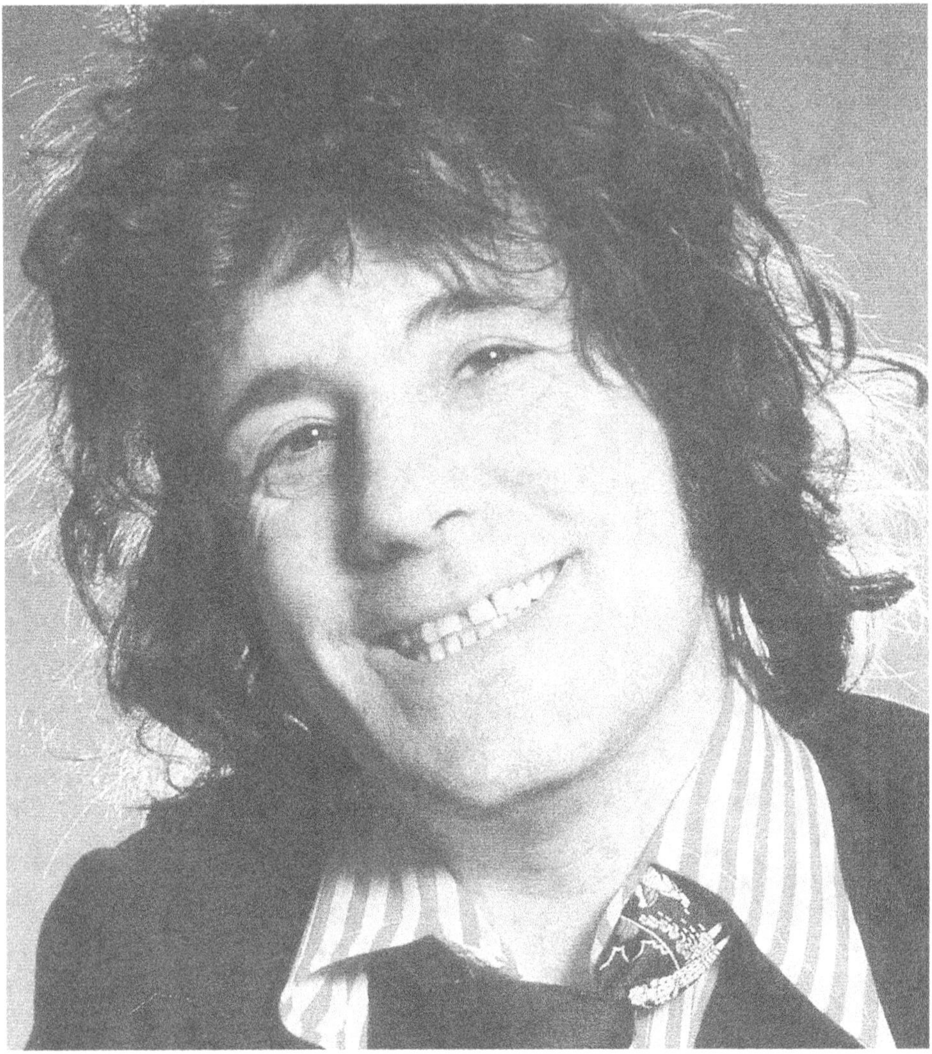

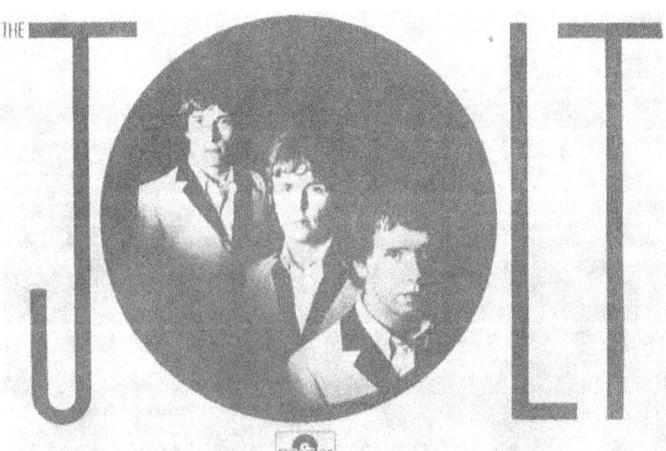

Above: Alex Harvey

Right: The Jolt

I didn't have the equipment either. I think if it came round again I'd have kept it as a three-piece – you have the equipment for it these days.

I'm a very lazy player, as you know – I can't be bothered playing chords and stuff, so I'd always be looking out for hook-lines and melodies to play, because they're much easier to do and more difficult to fuck up. So the thing is, if you have a nice strong melody, it's natural to add a harmony to it. And that's really how the Lizzy double-guitar came about. After that we just kept saying, 'Remember what we did on that song? Let's try it on this song now.' It does have a very Gaelic, Celtic thing about it. Phil's writing was very warm and personal so it's not a surprise the playing went that way too. I mean, I can't speak for Scott Gorham, being a Septic, but for us Scots and Irish it was true...

That's right, Alex – burn the place down
Harvey versus Celtic Park and The Who

THE SUMMER of 1976 proved to be SAHB's greatest period. Despite having just completed their own UK tour, they were added to the Who's four-date stadium trip to top up ticket sales. Normally promoters wouldn't touch a band who've just been out, because only a small percentage of fans will want to see them again so soon – not with SAHB. The jury's still out on whether they or the Who were the best band on the nights.

DAVID BOYES: When they played Parkhead, it was the first time a lot of Rangers fans had ever shown their faces there – things still ran deep back then. Alex was telling all the bands they'd better not be shite because he had four hundred cousins in the audience. Then, just as SAHB started, a big cloud of smoke wafted across the pitch, and some bluenose shouted, 'That's right, Alex – burn the whole place down!'

CHRIS GLEN, SAHB: This is one of my favourite stories, which I tell even more often than the other ones... Harvey Goldsmith was promoting, and he'd arranged for 30,000 salads to be on sale at the show. I told him, 'This is Glasgow; put on pies and Bovril!' But he went with the salads, and he had 26,000 sitting at the end of the day. He left them in Celtic's boot room – can you imagine what it must have been like when they went in at the start of the season?

Starting with a jolt
Punk travels north... a little slowly

THERE'S no doubt punk – the real actual what-we-all-call 'punk' punk – was a revolution and it did sweep almost everything away in its path. Like the skiffle and beat revolutions, punk reminded a largely-catatonic young population: *you* can do this; it's for *you*.

The revolution came in mid-1976. Chart-toppers included Slik's *Forever and Ever*, Marmalade's *Falling Apart at the Seams*, Tina Charles' *I Love to Love*, Brotherhood of Man's Eurovision *Save All Your Kisses for Me*, the Wurzels' *Combine Harvester* and the Real Thing's *You To Me Are Everything*.

But none of that was the news – by this time the music press was buzzing about the Sex Pistols. It was a buzz that, certainly in the beginning, didn't mean all that much up north. There was a certain Englishness about the whole thing that meant its take-off in Scotland faltered. But once we'd worked out our own angle on the new and very good idea, we ran with it – although, at brass-tacks level, we were all being Jock Tamson's bairns.

IAIN SHEDDEN, The Jolt: Our first pub gig was at the Crown Hotel in Wishaw and we played to exactly zero people. Now and again one of the long-hairs from the pool room next door would stick his head round the corner to check out where the almighty din of two-minute punk delights such as You're Cold and Responsibilities was coming from. Then he'd shake his shaggy mane and bugger off back to his game and the Eagles on the jukebox. It was bad enough having our passion, commitment, frenzied delivery and rage against conformity ignored – suffering it to the occasional strain of Hotel California was a bitter pill to swallow. Still, within weeks they were queuing around the block. A little victory, but an important one.

We weren't daft boys exactly, but we were incredibly naive and signed to Polydor, who immediately set about cloning us in the manner of their success story, the Jam. We did three British tours with them, dressed in similar suits, copping it from the press for being Jam wannabes. In truth we were a different kind of band, but we allowed ourselves to be moulded into something we weren't, and that was ultimately our undoing.

Bitter? Bollocks. The pointy end of those early days in Glasgow, vying for position with the likes of Johnny and the Self-Abusers and playing with the likes of the Jam, XTC and the Saints was life-affirming stuff. Clubs dripping with condensation and passion and raw energy and sex and you at the centre of it, living the dream and imagining it going on forever.

I remember the Jolt being banned from the Burns Howff when we'd only done a handful of gigs, after the *Evening Times* ran a story about us being a threat to civilisation. I also remember schoolboy Edwyn Collins coming up to us at the door afterwards to tell us how disappointed he was we couldn't play. Then there was the thrill of every record company in the country trying to sign us; me sitting on the stairs of my mum and dad's house talking to record producers and A&R men with Coronation Street going on in the background... My mum offering a selection of biscuits and cups of tea to punters who turned up at the door in binliners.

When we got to London we were beside ourselves, really, to be playing all of those places – the Marquee, the Hope and Anchor, the Nashville – that we'd romanticised so much in our heads while reading the NME, Sounds and Melody Maker in our bedrooms. That was the most exciting time... seeing the likes of Billy Idol or Chris Bailey or Siouxsie Sioux in the audience, there to see us, or in some cases just to be seen. We played the Marquee quite a few times and didn't always make it to the end. Spitting was always a problem, of course, made even worse when the gob was accompanied by a pint glass. I remember playing with X-Ray Specs there and lasting about fifteen minutes before it turned really nasty. It's best not to return the pint glass to its original user from the stage in these circumstances...

Various band members – including, I'll always remember, Doll By Doll's Jackie Leven – hustled our gear from the stage into the tiny dressing room before it could be destroyed. Same thing happened there with Generation X – and *to* them.

In a roundabout way my future was determined by the Jolt meeting the guys from the Saints when they first came to Scotland. We became instant friends, did quite a few gigs together and I ended up joining the Saints for most of their second phase in the 1980s, which in a roundabout fashion is how I ended up as music writer for The Australian newspaper in Sydney.

The Jolt was a means of escape. Like football, the armed forces and boxing in the old days, punk came along and offered the three of us a way out of the bleak industrial landscape that was Wishaw. Not to mention escape from predictable career paths and all the things we were reacting so much against, like people over thirty with long hair.

Glasgow versus punk rock
Councillor to the rescue after city tries to ban genre

PUNK was mainstream – except, of course, in Glasgow, despite a very successful Stranglers show. The ban had spread to Hugh Cornwell and co after a disastrous show at the City Halls; but the Glasgow Apollo management asked for another chance. The so-called City Fathers agreed, on condition that some of them attended.

BILL AITKEN, MSP: I will long remember the Stranglers concert. The City Fathers arrived at the Apollo to find an enormous queue of youngsters awaiting entry. Clearly there had been a lot of publicity surrounding the granting of the permission to hold the event – along with the stern warnings about the consequences of any bad behaviour. The kids were extremely pleasant and there was a lot of enjoyable banter.

We entered the theatre and were taken to a room in which there was enough drink to float a battleship. I got the impression the promoters wanted us to have an enjoyable evening – and wouldn't have been too concerned if we never left that room! Adopting my usual Cromwellian approach, however, I think I had a beer, then took the members out to watch the performance.

When the Stranglers came onstage they played one number, then said, 'Before we go on any further, where's Mr Aitken and his mates?' We stood up, and there was considerable applause, punctuated by some good-natured booing. The concert then proceeded and there was absolutely no trouble in the hall at all. It was partly to do with people having to stand at their seats, whereas in the City Hall they could mill around and get themselves into possible conflict situations.

At the end of the concert we went into the dressing room, and we had much good-natured banter with the Stranglers – who were much smarter than they would have you think. We parted good friends. I told them that they could come back any time, but that they wouldn't be allowed to perform in any hall where the layout was not conducive to good order. The Apollo was, in fact, an ideal venue.

As we left there were still hundreds of kids milling around, again behaving themselves just as kids do, with absolutely no hassle. They were genuinely very appreciative that we'd come to the concert and had been prepared to allow the Stranglers another chance. Believe it or not this is a great example of how city government should operate – and it's provided a host of laughs ever since!

Life in a Blair Street cell
Underground music... made underground

ROBIN SAUNDERS: If the Edinburgh punk scene could be said to have a heart, it would have to be the Blair Street practice rooms. Not a healthy heart by any means: its arteries were clogged with the grime of centuries and the accumulated sinking damp of the city's spectacular rainfall. To spend time there was to guarantee a respiratory complaint and, for the hypochondriacs among us, fear of bubonic plague.

I wound up playing bass in Badweeks, sentenced to several evenings a week in a Blair Street cell. In the Lord of the Rings trilogy we're never shown the dwelling-places of the Orcs… but I have a bank of mental images to draw on for that.

Our next-door neighbour was Mike Scott, then there was the Freeze, responsible for a couple of classic early punk singles of the kind which now fetch funny money on eBay from deranged Japanese collectors. Singer Gordon Sharp's haunting voice would later grace the first This Mortal Coil album, preceding his rise to international subcultural celebrity of sorts under the name Cindytalk, sadly still without honour in his own country. Late arrivals on the scene were an outfit by the name of Blak Flag – note the missing 'C' – so nothing to do with Henry Rollins' hardcore heroes. You'd recognise the guitarist and drummer as those bespectacled twins who went on to unlikely stardom as the Proclaimers.

On band nights I was usually the first to arrive. Solitary in the cell, munching chips on top of my bass combo, listening to the latest tractor production figures from Minsk on Radio Moscow, which the amp seemed to pick up very well…

Electricity was metered, so maintaining a continuous supply required careful forward planning. We were regularly plunged into darkness and silence, then by a fumble for coins with cigarette-lighter torches. When the coins ran out you could always repair to a communal area where there was a drinks machine supplying water – not quite hot enough to soften a PotNoodle, but we ate them anyway. There was also a jukebox, surprisingly lacking in punk records and on which we often took great delight in pissing off the serious types – Joy Division fans, mostly – by playing Captain Beaky over and over again.

There was rodent population too. After a night on the town, too drunk or too lazy to struggle home, you could spend the night in Blair Street… if you were feeling brave. Try to claim the pool table – they can't climb up the legs, can they? Try to drift off to sleep accompanied by the patter of tiny feet…

A riot of their own
Apollo bouncers earn their reputation

THE ARTS COUNCIL had a remit to support artistic endeavours which couldn't make money. It was possible for the Glasgow Apollo to make money because people wanted to see its bands, and therefore the Arts Council couldn't help keep it open as it teetered on the edge of closure in 1978.

The same month that bad news was shared, the body managed to help an American artist put on an exhibition of blank canvasses – an event which didn't stand a chance of being profitable because no one could possibly want to see it. That's our money they were spending, folks.

Asides from a rather disappointing gala night, where no big-name act in the world was available, the last show in the Apollo was the Clash. A recipe for intrigue, to be sure, which results in a nice big riot and several arrests, including the band's Joe Strummer and Paul Simonon. The story goes that the infamous Apollo bouncers were looking for an opportunity for one last big barney before they had to find other employment.

JIM WYPER: The atmosphere that night was very bitter. The bouncers have to answer for that. I remember the unnecessary provocation they were giving us as we went in. They told me to take off the chain and padlock I had round my neck, but I didn't have the key and the chain wouldn't fit over my head. They told me I wasn't getting in because it was an offensive weapon – how could it be when I couldn't get it off? Soon there were about fifty of us in the same boat, but there was a decent big bouncer and he managed to open our padlocks with a wee penknife.

You could feel the tension as soon as you went into the hall. The bouncers were just out to give us a hard time. *Anarchy in the UK* came over the tannoy and punks were jumping around as if a shock current had gone through their seats. It was brilliant! But the bouncers took it as a cue to start flinging everyone out. It was a shame, because most people were just having fun. After that they didn't let up all night – taunts and comments. Even during the show Joe Strummer kept asking the bouncers to leave people alone. They really earned their reputation that night.

COLIN MILLEN: I wasn't there, but I worked with a guy who'll die happy because he got the jail with the Clash that night!

It could have been a poor epitaph for the great Glasgow venue, but as it turned out the Apollo would rise from the ashes one more time.

Thanks, Teabag
Street gigs and the phantom reviewer

ON THE SLIGHTLY less bonnie bonnie banks of the Clyde, at Glasgow's Customs Quay House, there can still be found the remains of a bandstand.

The wood-slatted seats are all rotted and you'd get a nail up your bracket if you tried to sit there; and the stage roof is long gone. But back at the end of the seventies, it was a hotbed of young musical activity, and just about the only place you got away with playing punk in the city.

JOHN McNEILL, The Zips: We did two singles and both got good airplay from Brian Ford on Radio Clyde and John Peel on Radio One. We played everywhere, but we wanted to reach the under-eighteen audience, so we started doing Saturday lunchtime gigs at the Customs Quay House bandstand.

It was the place to be seen, mainly because Brian plugged the shows heavily on his Streetsounds programme. People would write in every week and give him reviews of the last show. One name in particular, Teabag, used to crop up all the time. Everyone thought it was me just trying to plug the Zips, but it wasn't... He used to put a used teabag in the envelope, hence the name. Good thing he wasn't called Condom! I often wonder who he was and whether he's still around.

Indie-schmindie
An alternative to punk: hideous inverted snobbery

JUSTIN CURRIE, Del Amitri: When I formed the band at school we were into the Gang of Four, Wire, the Fall, Buzzcocks, the Undertones – pop melody inspired punk, essentially. Our key album was *Dragnet* by the Fall. In our pathetic middle-class punk sensibility, we were pretty antipathetic to the trendy new wave bands on the Glasgow pub circuit. People like Endgames and Tutonic Veneer, we suspected, were punk pretenders who were actually just seventies careerists desperate for commercial success. Now, commercial success, or at least the abandonment of art to attain it, was total anathema to us. We were sixteen and we'd spent the last three years reading radical punk treatises by Julie Burchill, Nick Kent and Paul Morley in the NME – and even Dave McCulloch in Sounds. It was this generation, I think, which went on to form the loose indie-schmindie scene of the early eighties, characterised by a hideous inverted snobbery, a wilfully cute amateurism and an ironic attitude to rock.

Foul-mouthed Krankie
You always suspected... and you're right, there's proof

FROM the sublime to the ridiculous, and a quick reminder that music-hall entertainment wasn't dead either. One of the country's most successful exports at the time was the

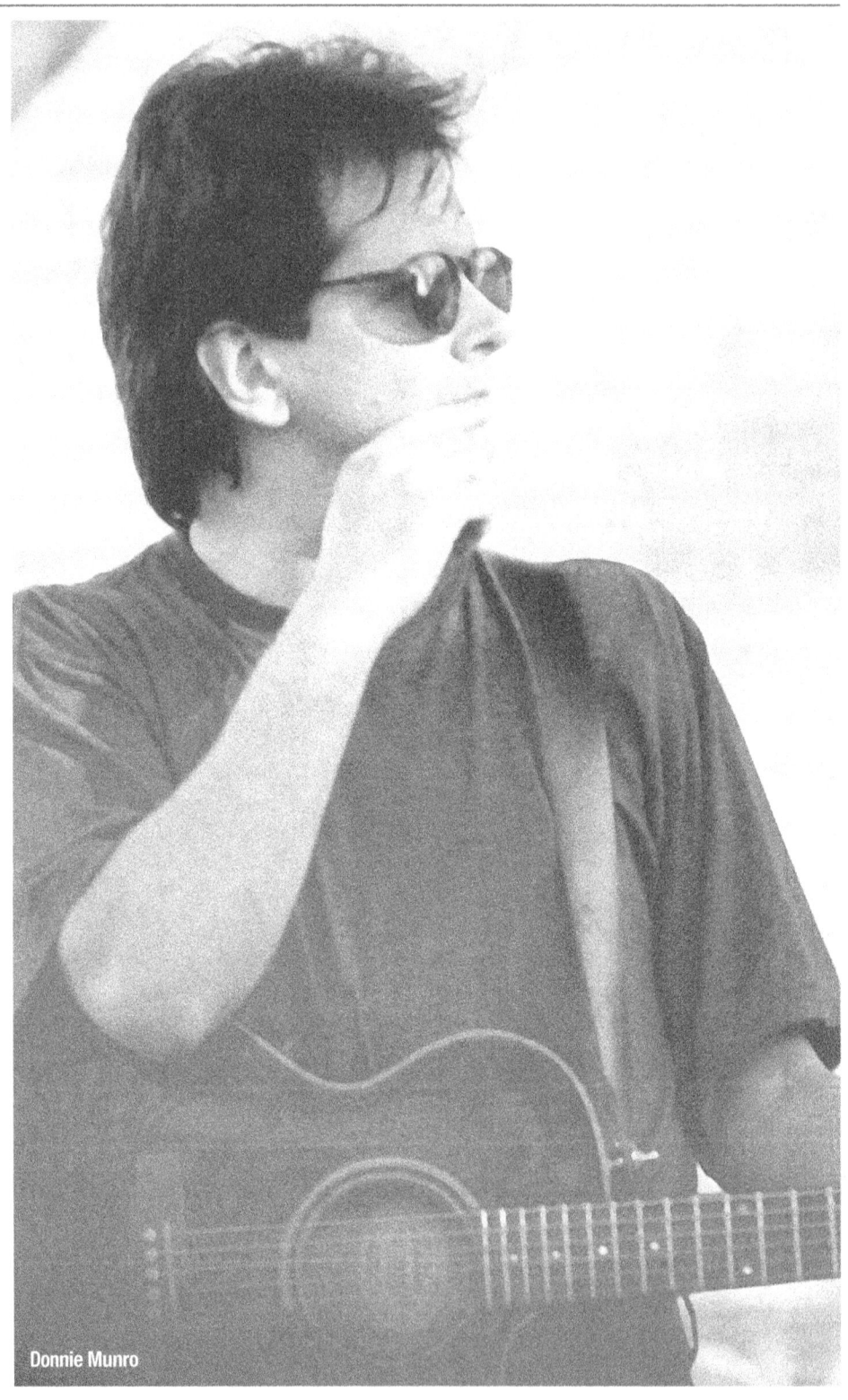

Donnie Munro

Krankies, the husband-and-wife Tough team, Ian and Janette, who masqueraded as Ian and Wee Jimmy. They presented Crackerjack, had their own TV shows and did tours and pantos endlessly. Let no one say it wasn't hard work – particularly when they had to squeeze in the recording of their album, *Fandabidozi*...

PETER KERR, Producer: Ian and Janette are a right pair of characters. I had to write most of the tracks on the album because the material just wasn't there; and they were dotting about on summer seasons and all that. We had to put down their vocals then record the backing tracks on later, which is the wrong way round, of course. It was hard for them, no doubt, but they're a pair of troupers.

Janette's got a good set of lugs on her but Ian's a wee bit slower on catching the melody, so we were doing the Fandabidozi track and Ian was lagging behind. Janette just said something to try and make things easier, and Ian said, 'Aye, alright, leave me alone...' and she said, 'I'm only trying to fucking help, c••t!'

Wee Jimmy Krankie using language like that! I kept a splice of it for years, in case I could blackmail them about it or something... The funny thing about that album is that it did okay when we released it here… but it made number one in Italy. The Italians went crazy for the Krankies!

Hidden history
Munro's rage over two decades in the dark

STUART ADAMSON had left the Skids and was beginning work on his grand vision – the result of which would be Big Country, of course. Meanwhile, in a similar but different vein of Scottish-oriented rock, Runrig's grandest moment came with their near-concept album, *Recovery*.

DONNIE MUNRO, Runrig: Obviously, we grew up with traditional music, but we pretty much rejected it at the time in favour of rock'n'roll. But when we all went to uni, we grew to appreciate those traditions because we'd been removed from them. So it was an easy decision to try merging those influences.

I suppose people tend to see us as a political band – but I don't think any band really can be. I mean, we were six people who could hardly agree on the bloody set list, far less any major political issues! But in the songs, and particularly on the Recovery album, we did focus on things like land issues, language and the right to self-determination within communities.

One of the most significant things for us was a song which translates as 'Twenty Years'. That's how long it had taken us to find out about our own social history. When we were at school there was just no reference at all to the agitation that took place in the late nineteenth century. We didn't know what our grandparents and great-grandparents had been involved in. There was this rage – why did it take me twenty years to find this out? There's a museum in Skye that I take my children to. It has an exhibition with a reconstruction of the Napier Commission, which was set up after the last land battle on British soil to look after the rights of the crofters. I discovered by pure chance that the man in the reconstruction, the central figure, was my great-great-great-grandfather! And I'd been going to the museum for so long with my kids, unable to point that fact out because it had been so difficult to discover...

I have a dream
The best World Cup anthem ever

SCOTLAND'S proudest World Cup moment came in 1982. Not on the pitch, of course, but in the studio. Who can forget waking in the night with a fever, when the sky was the darkest blue? John Gordon Sinclair, aided and abetted by the national squad, propelled BA Robertson's *We Have a Dream* to number five in the UK charts.

BRIAN YOUNG, CaVa Studios: The anthems were recorded at CaVa in 1982, 1986, 1990 and 1994. It was always a great buzz – especially if you're into football. It wouldn't be fair to say which one I think was the best – but we all have a dream...

We're all going to die...
You don't hit Hell's Angels
Robbo's short stint with Motorhead

THE EIGHTIES vibe was being defined by ideas as diverse as Duran Duran's *Is There Something I Should Know*, New Order's *Blue Monday* and Bowie's *Let's Dance*. Meantime,

CD players were introduced at the knock-down price of £450, Karen Carpenter died at the too-young age of thirty-two, Muddy Waters died at the too-young age of sixty-eight and Alan McGee formed Creation Records with a £1000 loan. Robbo, meantime, was winding up a short stint with Motorhead, in which he nearly got everyone killed, allegedly.

BRIAN ROBERTSON: I stepped in to finish their tour because Eddie Clarke had done a runner. How did it go? Scarily – very scarily... We did the Roxy in LA, and the Angels were doing security because they were all Lemmy's mates. We had a bus parked outside and I was going in and out, because I had to sit on the bus and learn the songs. Coming in new, they all sounded the same to me, so it was a job learning them.

So the Angel on the door had let me pass in and out all day. Eventually I got my ten-minute call and tried to go into the dressing room to tune up. This guy was out of his knickers by now, and he asked for my stage pass, and I said, 'Sorry, it's in the dressing room – but you know me.' He said, 'No – stage pass.' I'm this wee Scotsman with bright red hair and I've been going in and out all day!

I just said, 'No, come on, excuse me,' but he wouldn't move. I've only got ten minutes, so I thought, bollocks, and I nutted him. He just collapsed! Our roadie John had seen everything, and he's saying, 'Fuck's sake, Robbo, what have you done?' I said, 'Look, you deal with it – see you in a minute...'

So I got on with tuning up, then Lemmy comes in. 'What the fuck have you done? We're all going to die – you don't hit Hell's Angels! I'm saying, 'Look, he's not dead or anything...' I didn't even hit him hard... He wouldn't have fallen over if he hadn't been so drunk. If my dog had jumped up on him he'd have fallen unconscious – nobody was more surprised than me!

And that was it... no big deal.

Climbing to the Top of the Pops
Robbo's short stint with Motorhead

ORANGE JUICE and Aztec Camera enjoyed a great year in 1983. *Rip It Up* was the Juice's biggest hit, reaching number eight. As well as that smoother, mellower sound, Edwyn Collins' lyrics were decidedly more light-hearted and less political than those which had gone before.

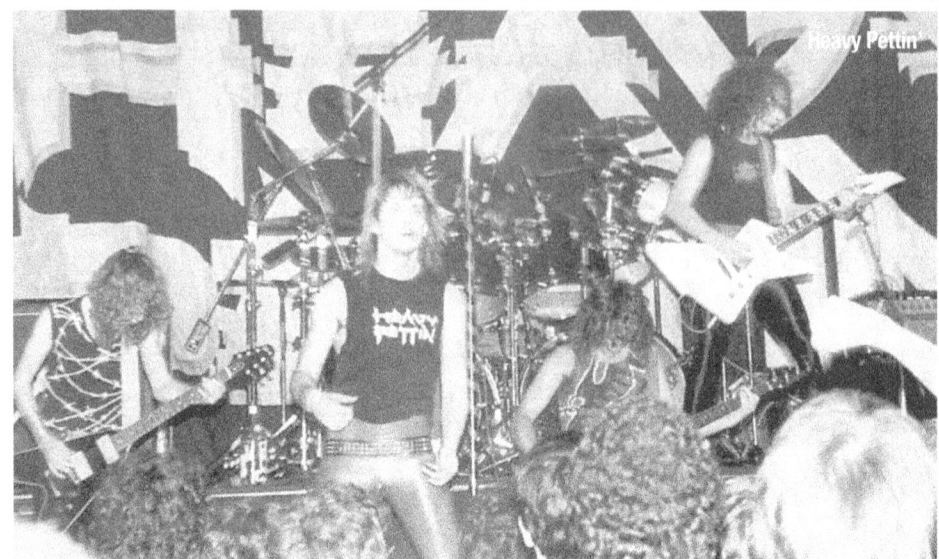

Roddy Frame and co's album *High Land, Hard Rain*, showed how they were also exploring a less cynical, jaggy feel. Speaking at the time, Frame said, 'I was sort-of bitter in a romantic way – I wasn't the best person to have at your party. But now I can cope much better. I'm more intuitive, and a bit more groovy. We're much more humorous and more confident on stage. I enjoy having a good time now – I used to frown on that.'

JOHN McNEILL, Passionate Friends: After the Zips we had a band called Passionate Friends, and we had one great year of nearly being stars. One of the top moments was on 18 June 1983, when we opened the show for Rod Stewart, along with the Jo Boxers and Gary Glitter.

It was a gloriously hot day and the crowd started to fill up the ground quite swiftly when the gates opened. We'd been tutored about how to move around and make grand gestures so the people at the back could see us. A whole different ballgame, if you'll pardon the pun, from our regular Sunday shows at Nightmoves on Sauchiehall Street. The punters were right at your feet there – here they seemed like they were a million miles away. The master plan to run energetically from one side of the stage to the other came to grief – we didn't have radio packs so we were restricted to running the length of our leads! But we were the only local band on the bill and the crowd got right behind us.

The Jo Boxers followed us. They'd had their hit, Boxer Beat, and it was the only song anyone knew. They kept themselves to themselves backstage – unlike Mr Glitter, who sashayed along the dressing room corridor, waving regally and lapping up attention from the backstage staff. We were all young boys – luckily we kept our distance...

When Gary took to the stage the audience went berserk. He played all the Glitter hits, and refused to get off at the end, which meant Rod and his band were late on. Not that they were bothered – they only arrived minutes before stage time, in a tour bus which drove up on the pavement outside the main door. They trooped in and went directly to the stage area. When they came off, they headed straight for the bus again. No contact with anyone backstage that I could see. Still, he did give the paying punters what they wanted. It was a great show.

Ian Donaldson's H2O enjoyed a season in the sun with the singles *Dream to Sleep* and *Just Outside of Heaven*. Veterans of the pub scene, they took their hard-earned musicianship down south and managed to make it work for them, even if it was for just a short time.

IAN DONALDSON, H2O: Having a hit record is equivalent to climbing Everest or walking to the south pole for anyone making popular music. And in the UK, appearing on *Top of The Pops* was like punching the air when you got to the summit of the mountain, or when you finally stood at the top of the world. All the years of playing every toilet up and down the country, of rehearsing and rehearsing and rehearsing, of listening to the records your heroes made until you knew every inspiring word and every sound they made... all of it was suddenly worthwhile. It's very satisfying to know that, no matter what happens next, no one can rob you of your place in pop history.

CAMPBELL FORBES, The Dolphins: Our best show was at the Kelvingrove Bandstand. We arranged it ourselves and it was a load of work. Even before the technical stuff we needed to deal with the police and the city council. We knew it was going to be a good night, but we didn't expect to sell out – four thousand people! These were people paying to see us, and listen to our songs. Local bands don't get that any more. It was a great night, and we even ended with a fireworks show – very special. I work with a lot of bands these days. It's a shame so many of them don't know how to work the gear they've got – I'd have killed for the stuff you can have in your bed-room these days.

Scotland's own oversized rock band, Heavy Pettin', scored a Polydor deal and released the album *Lettin' Loose* – a real Celtic take on the big-haired US sound. With titles like *Love on the Run*, *Rock Me*, *Shout it Out* and *Hell is Beautiful*... well, you know what you're in for, don't you? And if you can't enjoy it, FOAD, as we used to scrawl on walls.

PUNKY MENDOZA, Heavy Pettin': They laid it on for us – support slots with Kiss and Ozzy. I'd grown up listening to Kiss so it was a dream come true. Gene Simmons and Paul Stanley were really into us – there was talk of them producing and co-manag-ing us. That would have been incredible. And as for Ozzy... that's a book itself! Touring with Motley Crue was just a big long party. It was a pleasure to meet Brian May too – what a nice guy. He gave me a signed copy of the *Starfleet* album. It says: 'To Punky... it's partly thanks to you I committed this to vinyl'. That's yet another story!

Why would I join the Jesus and Mary Chain?

One-single revolution isn't for everyone

THE JESUS and Mary Chain's debut single exploded into life, and it was a real jawdropper. *Upside Down* featured a literally astounding feedback effect which blasted through the song. You either loved it or hated it – that one single was a mini-punk revolution.

BRIAN HOGG, writer: The great thing about the Mary Chain is that the base of their songs are classic American teen surfing tunes that have been ripped apart and stuffed with feedback. But once you get through that original noise you realise that they are just fucking great songs. But I have to say, it was the racket that originally attracted me!

DAVID 'GIBBY' GIBSON: I started playing bass late. Part of the problem was that most of my classmates from East Kilbride were highly accomplished musicians... Steven Lironi from Altered Images, who went on to produce Black Grape and, em, Hansen, and session muso Colin Smith, whose finest moment was, perhaps, the instantly recognisable bass line from Chicken Man, the original *Grange Hill* theme tune.

   I was approached by Jim and William Reid about the possibility of me joining their band, the Poppy Seeds. The songs they'd recorded on their Tascam Portastudio were good, but they were all acoustic guitar tunes. As a long-haired Van Halen freak, it didn't strike me as the sort of thing I really wanted to do. Along with many others I suggested a guy from our youth club, Douglas Hart, who seemed much more on their wavelength image-wise. He couldn't play! Of course, they went on to become the Jesus and Mary Chain.

I love my baby with a...

Billy Rankin's 'Kiss this guy' moment

BILLY Rankin had left Nazareth and tried his luck with a solo release. It worked out – the album Growin' Up Too Fast did fine, and he even had a hit in the States with *Baby Come Back*.

BILLY RANKIN: Towards the end of my Naz days we were being sent to more obscure territories, like Russia and Poland. One day, our agent called to offer us a week in Beirut. Nazareth in Beirut? Shurely shome mishtake... Zagreb had been cancelled earlier, because we couldn't get insurance for tank damage... But this? We declined the offer, and then asked, 'Why us?' The answer was, 'Because Boney M won't do it.' I chucked it not long after that.

Among the high points was becoming pals with Alvin Lee. He was one of my heroes – we used to play Ten Years After tunes in my first band, Phase. We were jamming at a promoter's house and I said, 'Gie us *Goin' Home*!' Big Alv pointed out he'd been gie'n us *Goin' Home* since 1968 and would rather French-kiss a skunk. 'Ah'll play it, then,' I said, and I did. And it was going well too, till I got to the second verse and sang, 'I love my babe with a rigorous arm... I love my babe with a rig–' 'With a rigorous *what*?' he said. 'A rigorous arm – y'know... phwaar!' I stuck my arm up like a big boaby. 'It's 'with a red dress on'!' he told me. Nowadays, when Alvin gies us *Goin' Home*, he alleviates the boredom by singing 'rigorous arm'.

BRIAN YOUNG, CaVa Studios: Recording Billy's album for A&M was our first serious outing with American musicians and an American producer. It's great to know there's a place in Scotland these guys were prepared to work.

BILLY RANKIN: My wife has never been over-impressed with the music business. I remember I came home from the pub and A&M had left a message. I called back to be told, '*Baby Come Back* has made the top forty in the States.' Brilliant – I shouted to her, 'I'm in the top forty!' She says, 'That's a lot of record sales... Who's buying it? That's the one you wrote in the lavvy, isn't it?' I used to keep my gold and platinum discs in there till she said they lowered the tone of the room...

Don't buy my single
Jim Diamond's heartfelt request

AS MADONNA arrived with Like a Virgin, Virgin Atlantic took to the air and the Tories' Brighton conference was bombed. Jim Diamond's songwriting achieved world acclaim when he was nominated for an Ivor Novello award for *I Should Have Known Better* and he achieved even more acclaim when he asked people to stop buying it in favour of Band Aid's *Do They Know It's Christmas?*

JIM DIAMOND: *I Should Have Known Better* was an idea I'd had around for a while. I eventually turned it into a song with Graham Lyle, and we knew it was good, and that we'd done the best we could with it. We didn't expect it to go to number one – you don't really think in those terms as a songwriter. You're just trying to do your best. It was a great feeling – but the best thing about it is you can keep on playing the music you love – you've achieved a certain amount of security. Money and plaudits aren't important, but the bills need paid and the kids need fed, and you need to think about that.

I thought Band Aid was a great idea – like a lot of people I'd seen Michael Buerke's reports from Ethiopia, and it seemed obvious to encourage people to buy that single instead of mine. I didn't think much about it – I'd honestly expect anyone in my position to have done that. In fact, I'm surprised more people weren't saying it...

BRIAN SALES: I remember seeing Jim on the telly, saying, 'It's great to be at number one, but next week I don't want anyone to buy it – buy Band Aid instead.' That's in-fucking-credible. Anyone's who's been in a band, spent years trying to make it then finally gets to number one knows what that cost him to say.

Wet Wet Wet? Sounds like a novely act...

Jazz band splits as fame beckons for some

GEORGE FUTTER: I used to do a jazz gig in a ruffty-tuffty venue called Broon's

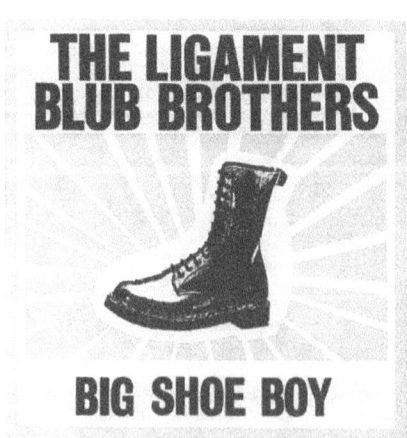

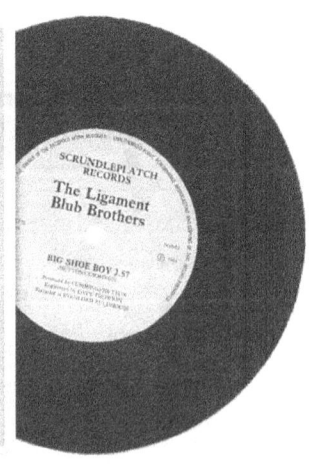

Bar in Stirling. It was organised by me and Bill Wells, the only Scottish musician I could truly call a musical genius. He's what you could call a 'band doctor' now – he's called in when you need proper musicality. Did some great work with Belle and Sebastian.

We organised the 'pad', as we jazzers call our repertoire, and some of it was very challenging... Charlie Parker, Zappa, Gil Evans and some original stuff. But we had no problems getting players, and it soon became a firm part of the jazz scene. Calling it 'jazz' is too small, though – sometimes it was out-and-out rock'n'roll. Sometimes there was a five-piece horn section, and there was always a strong element of funk.

We had plenty of major players dropping in – Duncan Findlay, Graham Brierton, Kennedy Aitcheson, Fraser Spiers, Bruce Adams. Guys visiting from London would want a piece of it too. But the main attraction punter-wise – and if I'm honest, personally – was seeing these major players getting their musical arses felt! Especially when it was by me, a violinist, whose instrument is constantly ridiculed in both jazz and rock circles. Those nights made up for some of the kickings I got at school for playing the violin...

We had a couple of young pups from Glasgow in for a while – Graeme Duffin and Ewan Vernal. They got through it pretty well – the boy Duffin, I thought, had the makings of a good player.

But one night they both came up to me and said they were leaving the band. Graeme had been rehearsing with a mob from Clydebank called Wet Wet Wet, and Ewan was with another band, Deacon Blue.

'Well,' I said, 'I can't see a band with a name like Wet Wet Wet going far – I mean, what's it all about? They sound like a novelty act or something... And as for Deacon Blue – what level of plagiarism is this? Man, they've even pinched their name from a Steely Dan track!'

Even worse, they were leaving that night, which was well short notice for a gig we were doing at Stirling Uni that Thursday. I wished them luck, but told them to keep their options open, and I hoped they knew what they were doing. And, yes, as they left that night, I shouted after them, 'The money ain't good in this gig, but at least it's steady!' Honest, I was half joking – but I did say it!

Then around twenty-three years passed. I was doing the Fred MacAulay Show on Radio Scotland with the Hugh Trowsers Band, promoting our single Living the Dream. During the phone-in bit Fred announced, 'We have Graeme Duffin from Wet Wet Wet on the line! To what do we owe the honour?'

Graeme's voice came through, 'I just wanted to say hello to George Futter...'

'How's it going, Graeme? Been a long time,' I said.

'Aye, hiya, George – I just wanted to phone and apologise on behalf of myself and Ewan for leaving you in the lurch for that gig a few years ago...'

'Aye, ye'r awright man,' I said. 'Water under the bridge now.' Fair made my day!

My hero offered me a beer ... and I turned him down

Fan starts fight for Lloyd Cole

SMOOTH soulsters Love and Money were next out of Scotland's bag with a debut album *All You Need Is Love and Money* showcasing intelligence, style and careful confidence. Remembered for sensitive acoustic guitar and an understatement that belied their attention to detail, singer James Grant and co were one of those 'wee bit special' moments that, sadly, didn't make the big time – but could have easily been eggshelled by it anyway.

CLIVE YOUNG: I'm not Scottish – I'm American and I've never even been to Scotland, but in the eighties it seemed like great bands were pouring out of the country... Aztec Camera, Lloyd Cole and the Commotions, Simple Minds, Big Country, Deacon Blue, the Blue Nile, APB, Altered Images – and, in particular, Love and Money. They all made Glasgow sound so exotic – they sang about rain and drinking. We had that here, only our city's musicians just got hooked on cocaine and killed themselves.

I was in university, and I'd become a writer for the campus newspaper. I saw in *Village Voice* that the band was going to play the Palladium in Greenwich Village. That was awesome! Then I saw the bad news – the concert was scheduled for the night before three final exams. If I went, I wouldn't get back to campus until at least two in the morning. Worse, I was already scheduled to work from four until eight in the morning on exam day. Going to see Love and Money would be nothing short of academic suicide. Naturally, I went!

The room held maybe two hundred people tops. There were a lot of industry folks there, mainly because Mercury hadn't bothered to promote the band – so the label workers had to show up at the gig to make it look like people came to the show.

The opening act was a ragged garage band called Too Much Joy – they were great. They were a horrible match for Love and Money, but for me, they were fantastic. Their only problem was their parents were in the audience and really standing out – so to hide their embarrassment the band had all been drinking. Before long they were ruining songs and making jokes that came across very badly. They were still a good band, though.

Then I spotted Lloyd Cole at the bar. Damn! I mean, *the* Lloyd Cole, one of my all-time favorites, here, in New York! I went over to bother him. It turned out he'd come to see the show and hang with Bobby Paterson, Love and Money's bassist. He offered to buy me a drink. I was in awe – my hero wanted to buy me a beer. But with three finals the next day and still being under twenty-one, I turned him down. I still kick myself about that...

I asked him what he'd thought of Too Much Joy, and he said, 'Ha – the world's got a Replacements... we don't need another one!' Two things happened then. I realised your heroes weren't always right about everything, and a friend of the band overheard the conversation and must have told them something like, 'Lloyd Cole's in tonight and he says you suck!'

I noticed a little later that some of the band were standing round Lloyd, and they were having an intense chat. I thought, good, they're getting some pointers from a professional – what a nice guy for doing that. But when I spoke to one of them later, he said, 'We heard he was talking shit at the bar, so we went and had some words...' Great! Trying to hang with a hero and I'd started a fight instead...

Love and Money finally came on, and James Grant greeted the cheers by saying, 'This is a very special night for us on this tour of America. That's because there's people in the audience.' The crowd had reached its peak of maybe eighty people in the place, so it was easy to walk up to the stage, where I watched in awe for the rest of the show. When it was all over, I was happy, exhausted and satisfied. It may have been cliché, but I had indeed been rocked. I got in as expected around two, slept for two hours, got up, went to work, then hit my three finals – which I passed with flying colors, much to my amazement.

As it turned out, Love and Money never played New York City again. If I'd skipped the show, I'd never have had the chance, the honour, the luxury of seeing them live. Lloyd Cole moved to the US permanently, becoming a fixture on the New York scene for a decade before moving to Boston. During his time in New York, if you knew which late-night club to stumble in to, you could find him jamming away with Brilliantine – a band that included the bassist from Too Much Joy.

The punk thing to do is split up

Anniversary party ends too early

DAVID 'GIBBY' GIBSON: I had a miserable time in London. I'd managed to join Mick Ransome's band by turning up the day before two hundred other hopefuls, and sharing a huge carry-out with them. It worked, and that was me in a band called Texas – stupid name, I thought. There were highlights – playing the Marquee, and having my song *Lies in Your Eyes* recorded in Trident Studios. I'd been in Sirrocco Studios in Kilmarnock, but this was the real deal.

Trident wasn't cheap, though, so I had no money to live on, and I nearly starved to death! Only the intervention of my dad, who'd just got a job in London and found me living in a dump in Braintree, saved me. I'm not kidding – I really was nearly dead...

I realised Mick really didn't give a fuck about anyone and quit the band. Mick went on to form the Tattooed Love Boys, who did okay. Back in East Kilbride, a dismal failure instead of the returning hero, I gave up playing altogether. Fortunately my mates Kenny and Cummy wanted me to join their band, the Ligament Blub Brothers. The idea was to celebrate ten years since punk – and since the songs were so fantastically out there, especially the outrageous lyrics, I was in.

We set up our own label, Scrundleplatch, and released the single *Big Shoe Boy*. For a while we were outselling the Mary Chain in France – we went top ten in their indie chart. John Peel kept playing it. Anne Nightingale, Andy Kershaw and Mark Goodier were all on our side too. *Sounds* wrote, 'A band so beautifully named, a band so fantastically East Kilbridey, what could possibly go wrong here? They could start singing, that's what...'

We loved it – because the thing is, while everyone thought *Big Shoe Boy* was an anti-fascist rant, it was actually about a barber we knew who had orthopaedic footwear. He stood corrected, get it? So did the DJs when we told them!

We did a live radio interview with our cocks hanging out, and the DJ didn't notice. We did the Arran Aid festival and went down a storm even though we were totally drunk. We did a gig in Blackfriars in Glasgow, where we thought it would get us some good press if a couple of mates sort of threw glasses at us. We made a mistake there – firstly, our mates got plastered and so we really did get glassed... secondly, we forgot to invite anyone from the press... and thirdly, why did we ever think 'Glasses Thrown in Glasgow Pub' could ever be a headline?

We started attracting major label interest, and Kenny and Cummy decided the punk thing to do was split up. So we did – much to my dismay, I must admit. Still, we had a good laugh.

Shit Factory
The trick is to keep miming

IT WAS 1987 and the revolution still hadn't come, so Stock, Aitken and Waterman staged one. The only other way to look at it is to accept their movement as the natural progression. If the folk who'd slammed rock'n'roll in the late fifties had seen this guff, they'd never have said a word against Elvis, Gene Vincent and those guys.

The rule was you picked up some good looking kids, you taught them a few dance moves, you found a song for them to just about sing and you put them on the treadmill, relying on their desperate desire to be famous and their youthful energy to carry them through. It was a packaging and sales job, and you told them: bank every penny, because you've got two years tops before nobody gives a flying one about you.

ANDY McEWAN: A lot of the road-crew work at my level had dried up. Blondie's tour had been cancelled because of poor ticket sales – I remember them saying it was the Rolling Stones' fault for charging £30 a ticket, back in the eighties... It took money out of other tours because people couldn't go to both. But some of the labels thought, 'That's it, our bands aren't doing Britain.' and that was it.

So I wound up working on a Stock, Aitken and Waterman tour – I won't say who it was. There I was, do-de-doo, do-de-doo around the stage.... Hold on, there's not a lot of inputs up here, is there? I've got seven mic stands, seven mics and one channel. Eh? One of the old hands must have recognised my expression – he just smiled and patted me on the back.

Come showtime, I just couldn't believe it! Everyone was miming. Everyone! The only reason they had one mic open was so the guy could talk between songs. Sometimes I thought he was singing but the old hand said they'd never let him – if the show sounded any different from the record, there'd be trouble.

I remember one Hit Factory act, who should have known better, getting caught miming because they stopped singing to say, 'Come on, crowd, let me hear you!' and her lead vocal kept going behind her...

Give me my money back
If they don't like your demo... charge them for it

COATBRIDGE had spawned cousins Ted and Hugh McKenna in the sixties, who became part of SAHB; and in the eighties the same town spawned the Kane brothers, Pat and Greg, who became Hue & Cry. They found themselves in a similar situation to the Wets, but dealt with it differently, accepting the challenge of making their musical ambitions match their label's requirements. *Labour of Love* ably demonstrated their R&B leanings, making number six and immediately putting the onus on them to do better next time.

Pat Kane told the *NME*: 'The label's been completely honest with us – they told us we'd be presented as two desirable young males, and our masculinity was to be as important as the music. I thought, "Great – we can re-examine homoerotic imagery." But they said, "No, you're gonna be juicy boys the wee lassies fancy!" Still, *Labour of Love* started out as an anti-Thatcherite song...'

JIM BRADY: It's hard starting a band in a place like Cumbernauld – you're pretty far removed from any sort of scene. We were playing places where the audience were expecting cover songs like Twisting the Night Away – and there we were with a drum machine, singing songs about Thatcher and nuclear power.

We decided we had to put a single out, so my brother Johnny sold his motorbike, and I sold my record collection, and we brought out this single called *Animals*. It didn't matter if it didn't sell as long as it raised our profile – sure enough, we came to the attention of Craig Tannock, who went on to open the 13th Note, and we started to play places like the Shelter, and got to know a lot of Glasgow bands. We always did well in Edinburgh for some reason, and I think the Glasgow bands were impressed with that, plus the fact that we had a single out... even though it didn't sell in the end.

We got some decent support slots with people like the Shamen, and the Young Gods – they were a revelation. We realised we were like the yin and yang of each other. We were both playing kind of electro-metal grunge stuff, but with different instrumentation. We became really pally with them and they even namechecked us on some of their records.

Record companies started phoning us because they'd heard the name, but then they didn't like the material. I remember the head of A&R at Chrysalis phoned up, and said he was interested. I said, 'Have you seen the band?'

'No!'

'Have you heard our music?'

'No, but we've seen the name about.'

So I reeled off a list of bands on his roster and said, 'We're not like any of them.' He still wanted to hear us, and I'm like, 'Look, we made the record on a shoestring, I'm on the dole, and you expect me to send you a copy when you could have gone into a shop and bought it yourself?' I was really trying to put the him off in a nice way, but he kept insisting. I said, 'You probably won't even listen to it – we know how it is, but... okay.'

Five weeks went by and I heard nothing, so I sent the guy a really irate letter saying, 'If I'd asked you for a free record, you wouldn't have given me it, so you owe me a fiver for that single and the postage...' Lo and behold, he sent me a cheque for a fiver – no letter, mind you!

The best thing about that, other thanpissing an A&R guy off, was that in every press release afterwards we were able to say we'd had our single paid for by Chrysalis. I didn't cash the cheque – I've still got it...

Wilderness of mirrors
A difficult early show for Primal Scream

JOHN MARTIN: I masqueraded under the name Martin St John and I was the resident tambourine man in Primal Scream until 1987. At the time we were a jingly-jangly sixties-influenced pop group with a manic edge. We nearly died before it all got going, though.

We were to play the Boardwalk in Manchester, and just outside the city the driver decided we were going the wrong way. Next thing we know, we're upside-down on a dual carriageway, skidding in slow motion... When we finally stopped moving we all staggered out, and some sick fuck stops his car, takes a photo then drives away! What a cheek! Bobby Gillespie and I were worst hit, but we got stitched up and did the show anyway. The crowd had heard what happened to us so they were on our side all night.

Next night, we were doing the Splash One Club. All I remember is dropping a tab of acid before I went on – we were all blitzed, so Bob G decided it couldn't get any worse and we stormed into a demented version of Belsen Was a Gas... I was tripping out my tree as I came off, and I got lost in the mirrored backdrop – I finally managed to get offstage by climbing into the crowd...

We knew we were paying
Runrig learn from playing poacher and gamekeeper

DONNIE MUNRO, Runrig: We'd formed our own label, Ridge Records, purely because no one was interested in what we were doing. But we already had a substantial live following and that worked in our favour when it came to approaching bank managers. There was still a huge element of risk involved – there's something very daunting about hiring a huge ballroom, using your own money, and wondering if anyone will turn up...

The only bad time we had was the first time we tried signing to another label. They were called Simple Record and they couldn't have been more complex – in fact, 'dodgy' is the right word. They ended up flooring most of the bands they'd signed, and they'd have floored us too if we hadn't had that incredible live following.

When we signed to Chrysalis and re-released *The Cutter and the Clan*, we were at last with a company that cared. The experience of running our own label helped enormously – we knew things like how much the pressing cost, and how much to budget for artwork and so on. I remember first time we went down, they sent a limo to pick us up at the airport. A lot of bands would have been impressed, you know, 'Wow, we've arrived!' But we knew we were the ones paying for the car!

Guests of Her Majesty
Rocking in Barlinnie Prison

JIM BRADY: We did a gig at Barlinnie Prison once. It had been arranged that a couple of members of the very captive audience would get up and sing with us. I say 'arranged' and I mean it – the governor and a social worker woman had pre-approved the acts.

The first guy came up to do his own song on an acoustic. He got to the mic and said, 'I was going to sing a particular song but I've decided to do a different one...' You could see the governor starting to look a bit worried. The one he'd had approved was all about how prison had made him a better person. But the one he sang was about the lack of women in jail: 'Shagging's great, I love fannies...'

It was jaw-droppingly rude by any standards. Every part of the female anatomy was discussed. There were even a few German moments in there! We were trying to back him but kept having to stop with laughter... Everyone was killing themselves, guards, the social worker, other prisoners – everyone except the governor, whose face was like thunder.

The next guy who got up was built like a brick shithouse. He said he wanted to sing Leo Sayer's *When I Need You*, and we weren't about to argue. I'll never forget it – he had the sweetest voice imaginable. He was built like a pit bull but his voice almost moved me to tears.

Afterwards, we were invited into the governor's office for tea, and I said that I hoped the first guy wasn't going to get into trouble for his song. After all, he wasn't encouraging anyone to get violent or escape or anything.

But the governor said rules were rules, and the guy had to be disciplined. Then he leaned in and said, 'These people aren't like us...'

My hackles fuckin' shot up and the claws were ready to come out when Stu Who crossed the thirty-foot room in about two seconds and wheeled me out of it. I think he thought I was going to pop the guy and we'd get to stay in Barlinnie overnight!

Have a biscuit...
Big John Duncan feeds the crowd

1988 WAS a turbulent year in the headlines. As the acid house movement began, the Piper Alpha platform exploded and killed 167 people. Iron Maiden fans died at Donington's oversubscribed Monsters of Rock Festival, and even those nice Deacon Blue folk were bottled off at Reading. 'Terminal Man' Sir, Alfred Merhan (the comma is part of his name) began an eight-year stay at France's Charles de Gaulle Airport. Midge Ure left Ultravox and Fish left Marillion. Jean Michele Jarre's super-pompous giant megashow at London's Docklands went off alright, as did the one and only flight of the Soviet Union's space shuttle. The Netherlands, those forward-looking souls, became the second country to connect to the Internet, after the USA, of course.

Goodbye Mr Mackenzie signed to Capitol and re-recorded *The Rattler*, this time featuring the furious guitar of Big John Duncan, but still *those* lyrics which halted its progress at number thirty-seven. In a later incarnation as a member of the Gin Goblins, Big John explained how he'd never quite fitted into the band.

BIG JOHN DUNCAN: I went out in the middle of a song and started handing out biscuits to the crowd. I think they were Abernethies. The band stopped the song! They stopped the song, and they were like, 'What do you think you're doing?'

'Handing out biscuits – what does it look like?'

I nearly left the band after the biscuits incident. They really weren't rockers.

DAVID MILLER, Finitribe: Edinburgh seemed so grey in the eighties. The only colour came from JJ's, Valentinos, Nite Club and the fantastic Hoochie Coochie Club. I think I went there Thursdays, Fridays, Saturdays and Sundays – every week. All these colourful people would appear, people who were really into music. It really was a great time to be part of that.

We were booked to support a band called Sian, featuring Marc Bolan's wife, at the club above the Edinburgh Playhouse. I can't remember anything about the music we played but I do remember the presence of Big John – he was and still is larger than life...

I remember seeing him come up to the front of the stage, then he started shouting and screaming at us. He was legendary for his heckling, and he was livid – he *hated* us, calling us fucking faggots...

He started gobbing at us, and one of the gobs flew straight into Chris' mouth. He was immediately sick all over the stage. John was laughing his head off... Everyone was terrified of him, but a few years later we became friends and he's one of the loveliest guys I'd ever met. Punk's no deid!

No trace of irony
Del Amitir's smallest fan and their one-legged groupie

THE NINETIES ushered in what has been referred to as the greediest decade in world history – until more recent history forced a rewrite. The first McDonalds opened in Moscow and the Soviet Union finally collapsed. Poll tax riots raged in England – we'd already had it for a year by then, complete with the promise of paying £206 per year for the foreseeable future (eleven months, apparently).

Musically, Scotland's artists took two views: the fist or the finger. While there was a thoughful edge to a lot of the country's output, 'fuck it and dance' was an equally prevalent attitude.

Witness Del Amitri's number eleven hit, *Nothing Ever Happens*, which represented everyone's New-Year hangover and much more besides. Not only did it snapshot the thoughts that were on almost everyone's mind at some level or another – it sent them round the world as big juicy stars.

I should mention at this point that my wee brother Damien and I wrote a spoof of the track, which he still plays as part of his musical comedy set, and the chorus went like this:

What a world to live in, what a place to be born
The goldfish will float to the top of the bowl and be flushed down the loo by yer mum
And we'll all be steamin' tonight and greetin' tomorrow.

Eh? Eh? Good, eh?

JUSTIN CURRIE, Del Amitri: Anyway... on a US promo tour we met four members of the Patridge Family over two weeks and in four separate cities. David was very nice but Danny was a freak. We later heard he'd only recently got out of jail for cocaine possession, and doing something unspeakable with a hooker in the back of his car. It may not be true – but having met the guy I wouldn't put it past him.

We were once asked by a radio DJ to hang about for fifteen minutes after our interview had finished because Eugene, the night DJ, was our biggest fan. 'Honestly guys, he'll flip out to see you guys – he really is your biggest fan...'

Eugene arrived and he was a dwarf. No one at the station saw the irony in the words that had been used to describe him! Two of the band escaped to the parking lot while I was forced to contain myself, be pleasant, and sign things, and have my photograph taken with our biggest fan, Eugene. I've never forgiven those two band members.

On a similar note, we once had a famous one-legged groupie hang backstage at a club in Houston. In order to get some sympathy so she could hoover up our rider, she complained her boyfriend had stood her up... Here too, there was no trace of irony.

So Deborah Harry faxed Lou Reed

Hugh inspires one of his greatest fans

AYRSHIRE'S Trashcan Sinatras released *Cake* in 1990, an album which was to become viewed as a cult classic, in America at least. The band spent time trying to make their US popularity work for them, and it may have affected their standing at home. They're still one of the very few bands to consist entirely of top-notch songwriters, mind – *Obscurity Knocks* was a spiffing debut.

So too was *Six to Wan (621)*, the first single by Hugh Reed and the Velvet Underpants. Inspired by the Sensational Alex Harvey Band and improv-rockers Edith and the Ladies (whose frontman Max Maxwell went on to perform with SAHB in their twenty-first century reunion lineup), Hugh Reed O'Hagan put a band together and vowed to deliver songs about Glasgow in a Glaswegian style.

At the same time, attention was paid to every facet of performance that could be applied, resulting in a madcap style of entertainment you'd have to see to believe. Quick-change costumes, audience interaction, comedy sketches, cleverly arranged video playbacks and latterly burlesque dancers have all been part of the show.

HUGH REED: The idea behind the band was that, in the way Lou Reed sang songs about New York street life, we'd do the same about Glasgow street life. We've always been a predominantly original band, with just the occasional cover song, but the rise of the tribute band meant we were often mistaken as a Lou Reed tribute band. So we had to change the name, to the Hugh Reed Explosion, and now we're a tribute to ourselves!

We used to do a cover of SAHB's *Framed* and I used to run to a van outside and dress up as Jesus, complete with crown of thorns and full-size cross. It was always a mad dash getting back to the stage on time. One night, in my haste, instead of re-entering the pub I went into the restaurant next door... Imagine the faces!

The band liked to play the wrong song as I walked up through the crowd, so I'd be coming back on to Folsom Prison Blues or Jailhouse Rock... Last time I played it was at the Royal Concert Hall when we were supporting Deborah Harry on her 1993 tour. When I came in from the back of the hall people actually booed – it was a family audience and I think they misunderstood my intention. Someone did shout, 'Give us Barabus!' which I thought was quite funny.

The best moment from the Underpants was duetting with Deborah on the last night of that tour – we sang the Velvet Underground number *Waiting for the Man*, and Deborah faxed Lou Reed to tell him she was singing with Hugh!

Hugh Reed

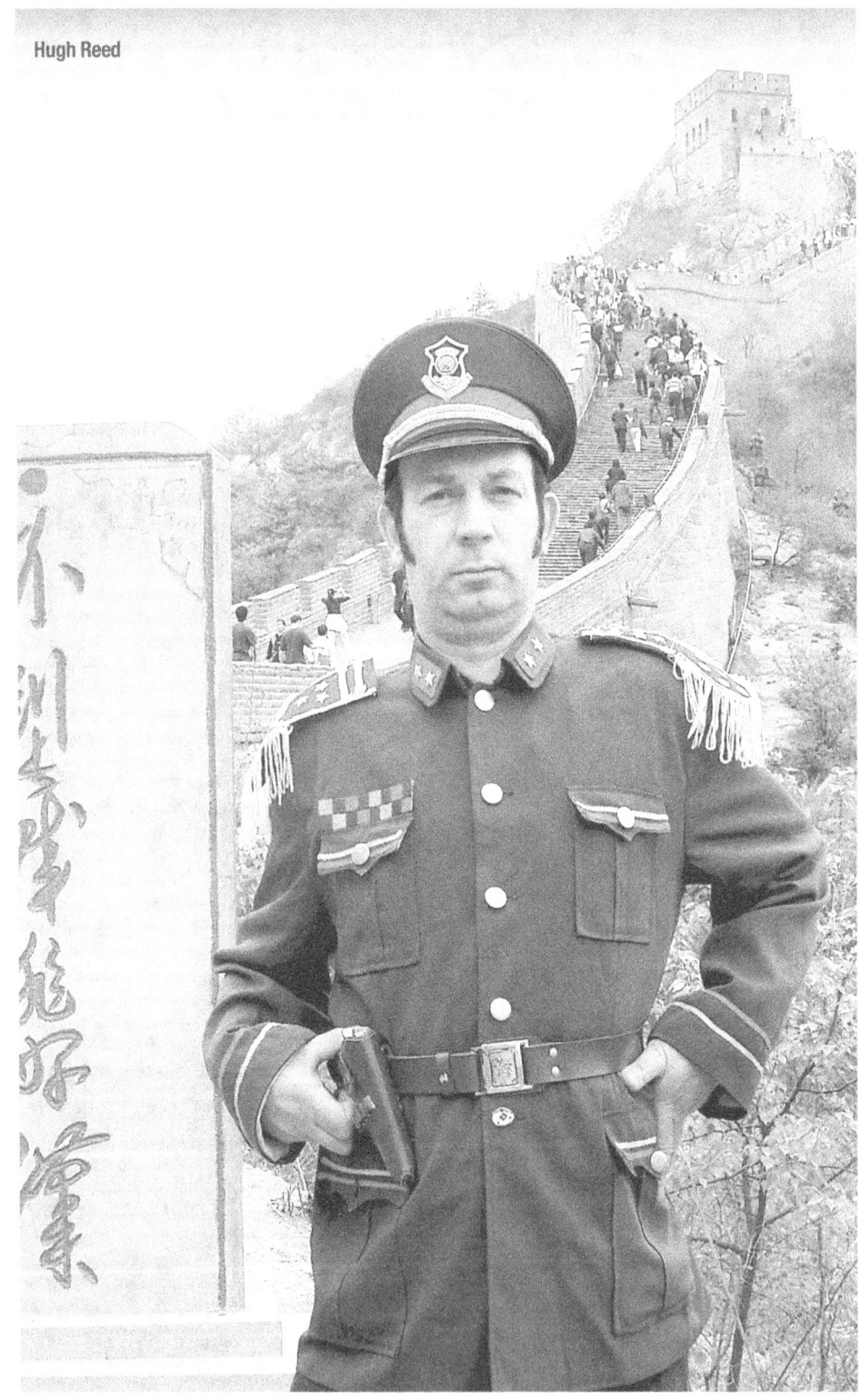

I didn't really understand who Nirvana were...

Vaselines suprised by superstar namechecks

WHEN Nirvana played in Edinburgh in October 1990, Kurt Cobain asked local band the Vaselines to get back together to open the show. He'd been a huge fan of their three-year career, and Nirvana regularly played two of their songs, *Son of a Gun* and *Molly's Lips*. For the band's co-leading light Frances McKee, it was not a grand event.

FRANCES McKEE, the Vaselines: Aha! The Vaselines again. I'm a firehorse... Apparently the Chinese kill us as children or avoid having us, as we can be extremely unlucky – or extremely lucky. You decide which one.

The Vaselines were a joke. It was hard for us to hold our heads high at sound-checks, or even at supermarket checks. We had no fans. Well... I had one. He cornered me in the laundrette while I was trying to stuff my dirty smalls into the machine. I never liked washing my laundry in public – then I went and dropped my pants trying to shove everything in too quickly.

I've only heard *Son of A Gun* once – it's never been my favourite song, so whatever anyone else did with it had to be a bonus. *Molly's Lips*, I can't even remember. I remember I had to give clearance for it to be put on a CD for children in America, and the guy asked if he could change it to *Mommy's Lips*. No problem, I thought – it would be nice for the toddlers to be singing not only about oral sex, but incest as well. Lovely. *Jesus Wants Me for a Sunbeam* was a big improvement, and sad as well.

We got back together for that show with Nirvana. It was a bit strange – we hadn't played together for a long time, I hadn't played my guitar for a long time, and therefore I hadn't rehearsed for a long time. The result was pretty bad; so I had to get very drunk to cover my embarrassment.

I'd been teaching for about a year and I'm ashamed to admit it, but I didn't really understand who Nirvana were. My dad thought the guy's name was Kurt Cocaine... but they were all really sweet. We only really started to have fun about ten minutes before we got kicked out of the venue. I don't remember the rest, but I'm sure I didn't vomit on my way home – miracle!

I have no memory of any of those Vaselines shows, except having bottles thrown at us in the Barrowlands when we were supporting the Jesus and Mary Chain. Again, we hadn't rehearsed. I bumped into Stephen Pastel recently and he said that gig was the worst one he'd ever been to. Anyway, the bottles got thrown back at the audience. Not nice...

Don't waste the film
Metal band wins talent show – no one cares

MARTIN KIELTY: By the end of 1990 I'd made a decision: it was the drums. I'd been in an all-keyboard school band, which I cringe to admit I called the Lords of Convention. I mean, how many ways can three words be so wrong? In my defence I'd just discovered a passion of Scots history, and I was trying to be, well, historic. But, no more synths for me – although I now own one of those (un)cool as fuck over-the-shoulder numbers, which looks (un)great on me. Nope… drums it was, because we'd discovered metal, and it was either that or bass. Me and string instruments had fallen out in primary school.

We called the band La Guerre – lager, get it? There were four of us unless we were doing a gig, in which case there were three because Alistair, whom we called Alice Dear, crapped out of gigging. Thus it was we became one of those bands to have the dubious pleasure of winning a talent show in our home town, Cumbernauld. Do not for a second think it was because we were good. It was because we were funny. As young lads, our definition of 'funny' was experimentally flexible, so that when I suggested we should shout 'Fix!' no matter who won, it didn't occur to me that the rest of them wouldn't shout it if we were shouting at ourselves. So I shouted 'Fix!' while no one else did and looked like a complete prick, as usual.

Still, there was no evidence… the local paper's snapper, who'd dropped by before the show, hadn't bothered to take a photo of us because, hey, we were a metal band, so we couldn't win. It's like a whole big Scottish attitude in one wee new town!

Shamen shame
The tragic death of Will Sinnott

RIGHT, on to things you might want to read about… In 1991 KLF hit with *3am Eternal*, the IRA bombed Downing Street and the Gulf War (the first one) ended. The Shamen released *Move Any Mountain*, which marked their crossover from an also-ran indie rock band to a global rave act. Tragically, founding member Will Sinnott drowned in Tenerife on a break from shooting the promo video.

MAX MAXWELL, The Shamen: Will and I were at school together but I didn't

The Vaselines

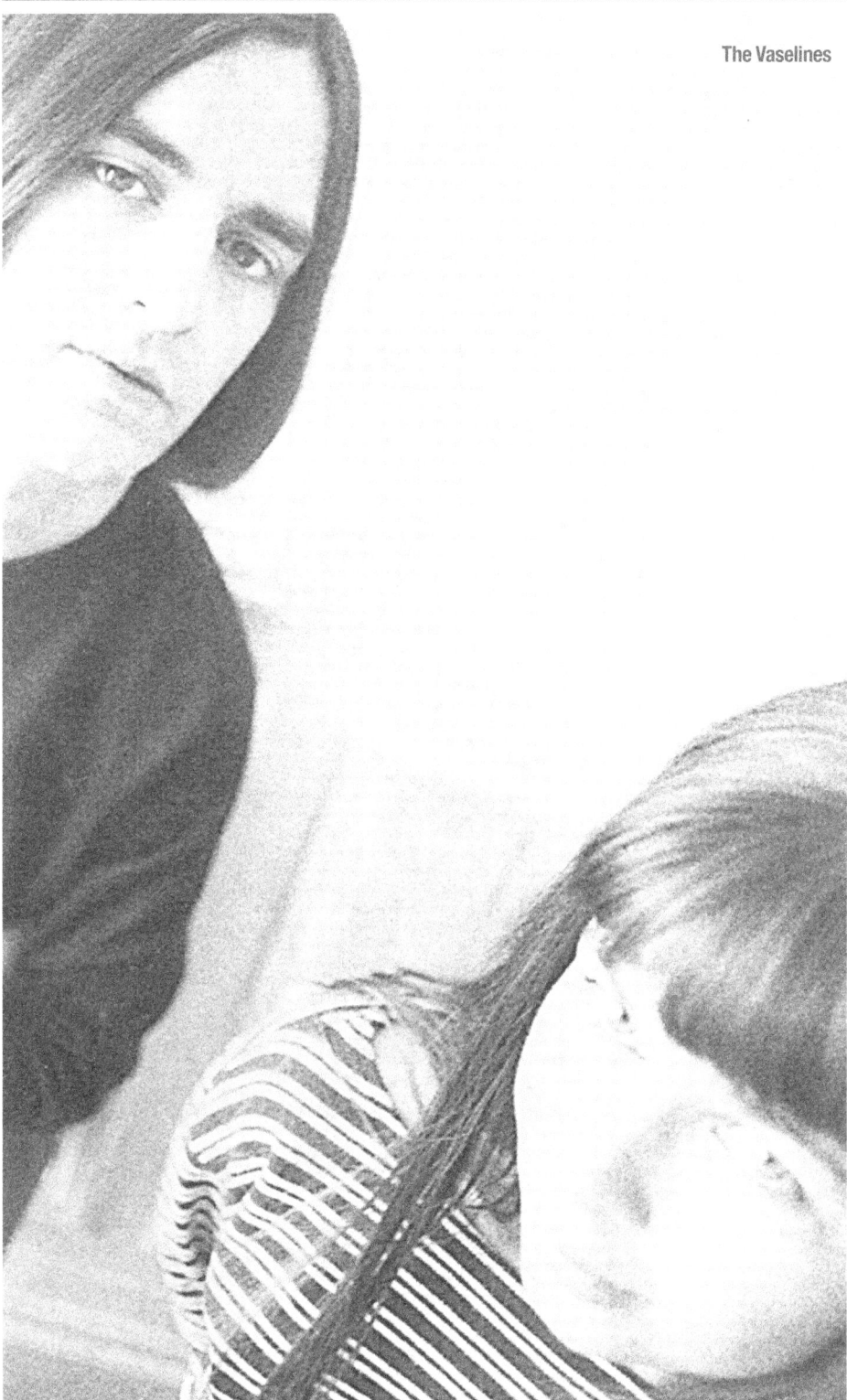

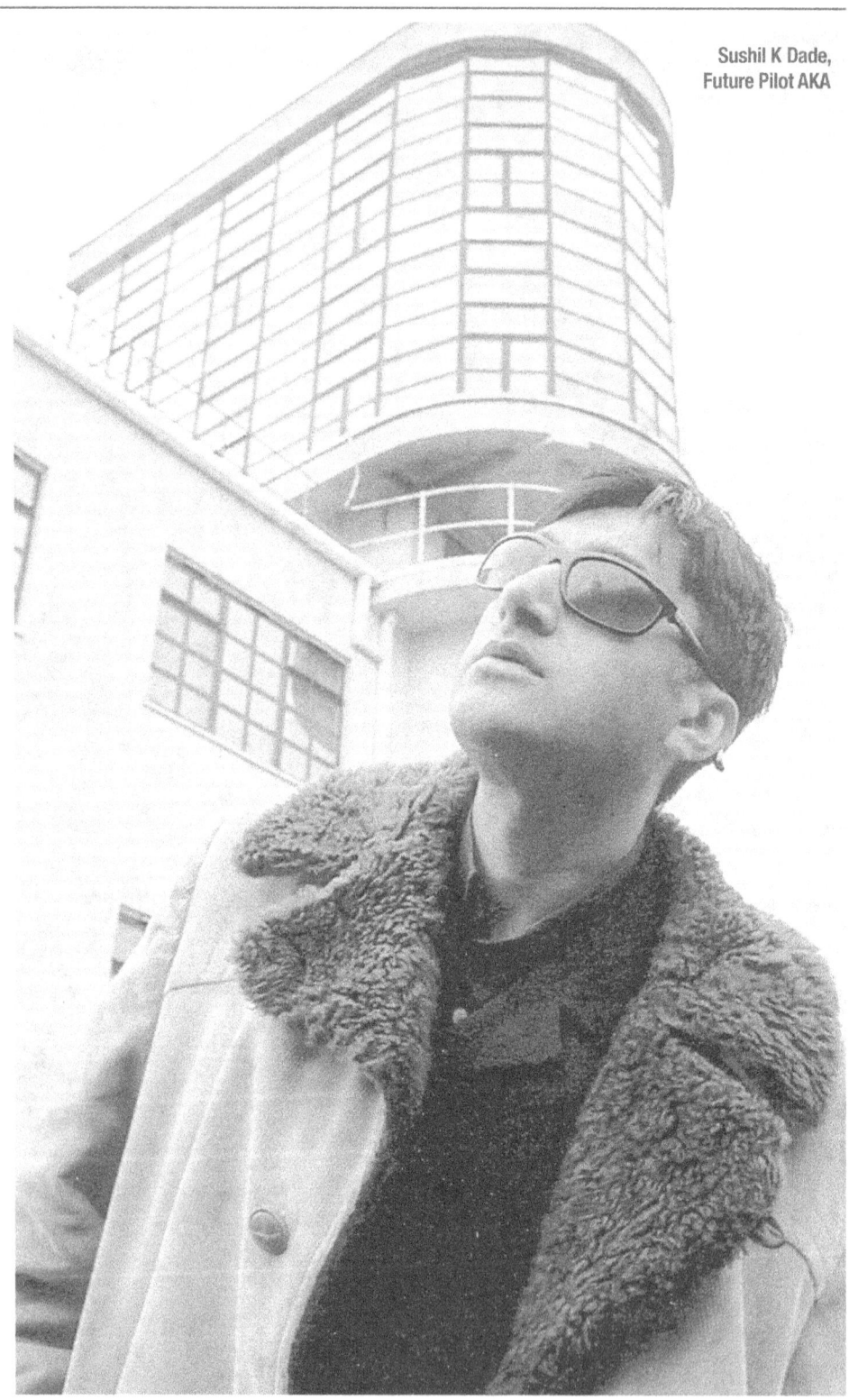

Sushil K Dade,
Future Pilot AKA

get to know him until I met him at a party just as punk was taking off. We had similar tastes in music – we were both influenced by SAHB in particular. In fact, Will reminded me of Chris Glen in his stage performance.

My first band had been called The – everyone else was *the* Clash, *the* Damned… we were just The. Then along with Will I started a fifteen-piece band called the Nolan Brothers, which was a pastiche of every style of music; we dressed up in costumes to suit what was being played. It was all very theatrical.

When I moved to Glasgow I used to drink in the Griffin and boast about how many bands I'd been in. One night, a promoter came up to me and said, 'You're in Edith and the Ladies, aren't you?' I said I was – it was one of the names I'd been bandying about but it didn't actually exist. He said, 'Great. You're playing at Joanna's next week!'

So I phoned Shug Carlin and Will, and we did the gig, purely by making up songs on the spot. We relied on our tape machine, Edith, to provide random noises like hoovers and car engines. It worked – we developed a cult following and lasted from 1979 till 1986.

Will moved to Aberdeen, met Colin Angus and joined the Shamen. We kept in touch – in fact, just before he died he was talking about a solo album with me doing the lead vocals for him. But his death devastated me. Will was a very special person – not just a great creative musician, but so fantastically intelligent as well. He could have been anything he wanted to be.

It wasn't a gig – it was a gathering of friends
1991, Runrig's greatest year

PRIMAL SCREAM'S *Screamadelica* was their breakthrough moment, showcasing the completion of their move to a genre-crossing music machine. The LP has been voted the best Scottish album of all time at least three times. Meantime, the BMX Bandits' record *Bandwagonesque* was that group's finest moment too, succeeding in generating a melting-pot feel and a whimsical production which warmly defined exactly what they were trying to achieve.

DONNIE MUNRO, Runrig: I'll never forget our show at Loch Lomond. It was just an amazing experience. I remember all these journalists backstage saying to me, 'Isn't it incredible, you playing to fifty thousand people?' But it wasn't – it hadn't happened overnight. We'd met every one of those people at village halls and clubs throughout the land over the previous ten years. It wasn't a gig, it was a gathering of friends, and that made it even more amazing.

We had a phenomenal year in 1991. Straight after Loch Lomond we did three sold-out shows at Edinburgh Castle, to something like eight thousand people a night. We invited the Gaelic poet Sorley Maclean to do a reading before one of those shows. Sorley was in his seventies and was used to doing readings to about three hundred people – but he did it. His amazing voice rolled out across this misty night on the castle rock... It felt as if the spirit of all the Gaels had come to reclaim the land.

Then we got hold of a circus tent and did a tour of the Highlands and islands, to crowds of three thousand a night. After that we did a spell in Europe and then came home in December for eleven sold-out gigs across Scotland. When I think about the percentage of the population we played to that year, it really is quite incredible.

Oasis wiped us out
Britrock versus Scotrock

WHILE Scots outfits with an established following could keep charting, the chances of a new band being signed reduced to near zero.

TAM, Barky! Barky: There's a classic story about John Ottway releasing a single with a scanned Supertramp album label on it, and he's scored out their name and scrawled his own over it. Warners phoned up and said, 'You're not on our label – we didn't sign you,' and Ottway goes, 'No – I signed you!' That's kinda how the Barkies' second single, Valentino, came about... It was saidflorence's money that paid for it.

JIM, Barky! Barky: It's true... Bruce Findlay started coming to our gigs – a lovely guy who genuinely liked the band, and even better, he actually liked the fact that I ranted between the songs! He'd just finished with Simple Minds and wanted to start a new label. He got two million out of Sony for saidflorence so he spent some of it on us – got us a couple of high-profile gigs, and put us in a studio with Callum Malcolm, who'd produced the Blue Nile.

The problem was the stuff we were doing was starting to go out of fashion. Oasis wiped us out. There'd been a brilliant time when you could get away with mixing up any kind of music, but when grunge and Britpop started happening anything with a drum machine was out of favour. It's a shame, because Bruce put a lot of effort in and so did we – but we were finished.

TAM, Barky! Barky: But I told Kit Cummings about using his saidflorence money. He was cool with it. Thanks, Kit!

SUSHIL K DADE, The Soup Dragons: We had a real blast making records. I really loved the tours where we had My Bloody Valentine open for us too. It was all pretty low-key but at least the Dragons had hotel rooms! The guys from MBV used to sneak in for a wash then head back to their Transit. Not glamorous – but it was pretty clear they would be big. They turned out to be one of the most creative bands of that period, and it was really special to witness that volcano about to explode.

A similar thing happened a few years later when a little unknown group called Oasis opened up for the BMX Bandits. We played in Worcester to about seventeen people, and I remember thinking, 'This band are going to be huge'. They already sounded awesome at those early shows – and they were all sweet guys too... don't believe the hype.

Touring the States with the Dragons was incredible too. We played everywhere from Hoboken in New York City to Madison Square Gardens, opening for INXS. Alice Cooper came backstage to say hello! We played at the club where Prince used to hang out and backstage that evening was a very hungry Alex Chilton, who cleaned up a fair portion of our fruit bowl – he was a healthy-living guy.

Hanging out with Dennis Hopper, doing the David Letterman Show with Darlene Love, touring with Tom Tom Club... Tina Weymouth taught me a lot about bass technique – she encouraged me not to use a plectrum and I've never used one since. She's an incredible bassist and storyteller.

We hid the 'H' so it still said 'Tongs'
Band name gimmick backfires

G-MAN: This is a great story when you remember King Tut's claims to be the king of cool... We'd added another guitarist to the band to give us a harder edge and decided to relaunch the band with a new name. As a bit of an old schemie I decided to use the name the Tongs. It was an old gang name, very well-known around Glasgow, and I admit I was hoping for some publicity out of it.

What I didn't expect was a phone call from Tut's boss Geoff Ellis, who was concerned that he might have a riot on his hands if we used the name. I thought, great – it's working!

I told him that since we'd hired the venue we could call ourselves what we liked, but he said he wouldn't let us play and we could have our deposit back. To say I was pissed off would be an understatement...

But a few days later I was in Sax in Cumbernauld and I saw an old poster for a Chippendales-type troupe of male strippers, with bits of string hiding the lads' nuts. A light bulb went on in my head – I asked the venue for the poster and took it home, then phoned Geoff and said we'd call the band the Thongs. But my old punk roots weren't going to let them away that lightly – you could barely see the 'H' in 'Thongs' because I hid it behind the photo of the male strippers.

Still, we sold a lot of tickets, and went on with *Saturday Night's Alright for Fighting* and covered *Do Anything You Wanna Do*. I'm pretty sure there wasn't a riot – although someone spilled a drink...

I was meant to be a primary school teacher
Pop gets in the way of Bis singer's real life

MEANTIME, the Delgados' early releases on their Chemikal Underground label set them up beautifully. First came their own single, *Monica Webster*; then came *The First Big Weekend* by Arab Strap, which then featured in yet another beer ad (well, Guinness); and next up, 1996's *Kandy Pop* by Teen-C heroes Bis. They jumped into the limelight when *Top of the Pops* producer Ric Blaxill heard the track and put them on the show. They're reputed to be the first-ever unsigned act to appear – although some people like to question that without providing a backup argument, and can therefore shut it.

MANDA RIN, Bis: I was 16, John was 15 and Stephen was 17 when we started. They wanted someone to play keyboards so they could concentrate on guitars so I decided to give it a go. When we did our first gig at the 13th Note, I was incredibly shy – I think I spent most of the time with my head down, just playing. Then I wrote

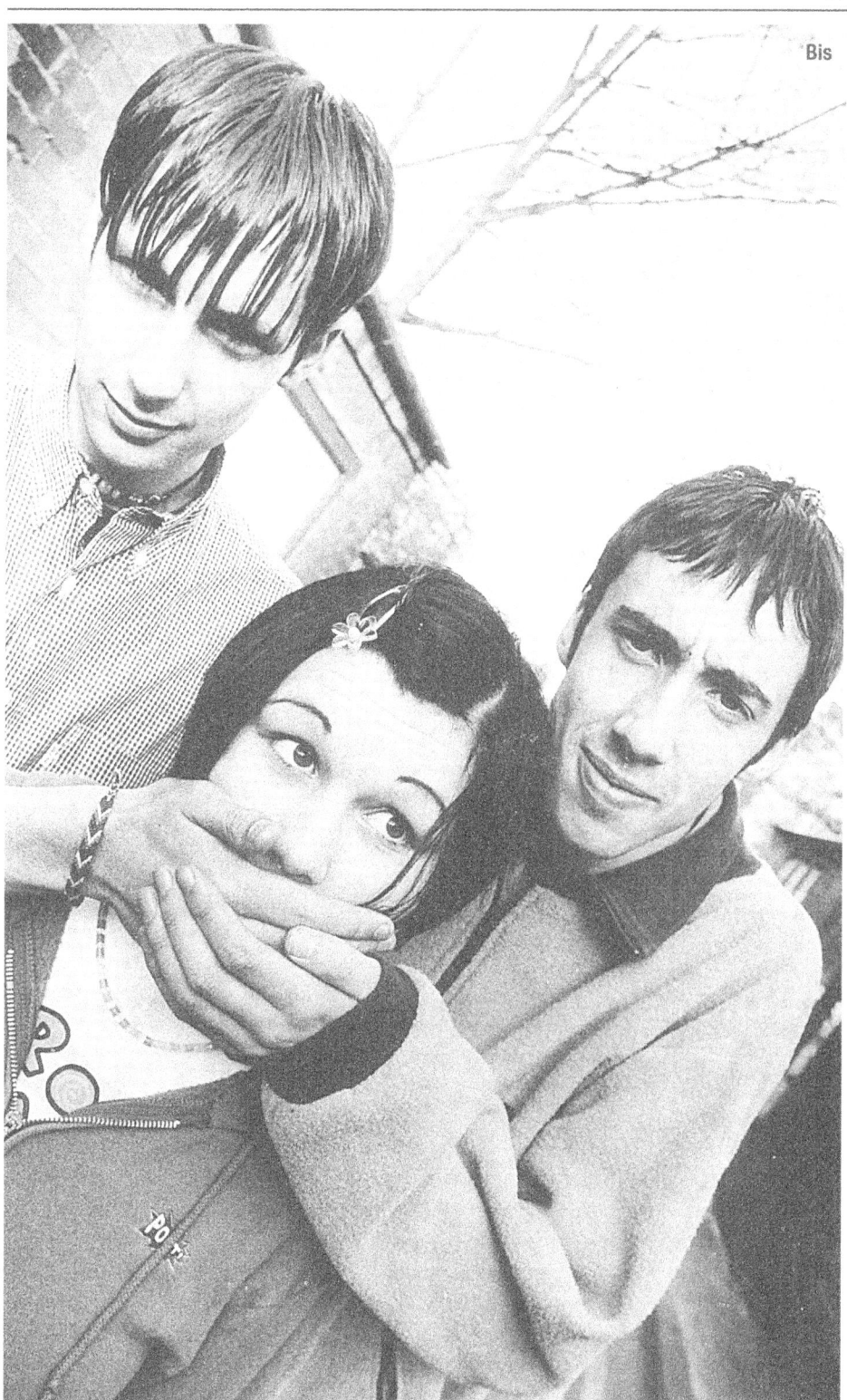

Bis

my first song and had to sing it... I was so shy I don't remember it at all, but everyone said it was brilliant, and I couldn't believe it.

That song, *Kill Your Boyfriend*, became our first single. We were writing fanzines, all those stories about the Teen-C revolution, and a guy from Spain thought he might like our song because he liked the music we wrote about. It was the first release on his label.

Things were going really well – John Williamson started managing us and he got us a four-week tour with Super Furry Animals. I'd just left school and I was supposed to be going to uni, to become a primary school teacher, but I decided to defer it for a year and see what happened with the band.

My mum was outraged – but it was a different story when Polygram gave us a £90,000 publishing deal... We lived off a tiny wage but we were still all with our parents so we didn't have much in the way of outgoings. We bought this tiny wee van and went off on tour with the Super Furry Animals. Half way through we got the call about *Top of the Pops* – the producer loved *Kandy Pop* and would we go on as an exclusive?

I found a video of the performance in my parents' cellar recently, and I can't believe how awkward I looked. My voice had started to go on the tour so I'd been taking honey all day – we didn't even have a drink to relax before we went on. I do remember the dress I wore cost me a fiver from Virginia Galleries...

Kandy Pop went to number twenty-five so we went back on *Top of the Pops* just as the tour ended. The difference in our performance was night and day – we'd really grown in confidence.

Home for hard-up hamsters
The veggie legend of the 13th Note

JOANNE PATTINSON: I was in the 13th Note in Glasgow and a couple of guys came in, really pissed, and started ordering bottles of champagne. They invited me and a barmaid who was just finishing to join them, asked us out and said they'd take us anywhere we wanted in the world. They said they'd just won the lottery, and they were really nice guys, but they got so pissed you couldn't talk to them any more and I went home. About two weeks later I was out and about and these two guys were all over the record shop windows – they were in Travis. They must have been spending their advance; I wonder if the barmaid got lucky?

CLAIRE SWEENEY: I worked in the 13th Note when it was in Glassford Street. Alex from Franz Ferdinand used to run a weekly gig called the 99p Club. I'll never forget seeing the Supernaturals... they were nice enough, fairly quiet guys – then they came on stage. The singer was wearing the maddest costume I've ever seen – his trousers and hat were all stars and stripes, and the whole show was amazing. They were one of the best bands I saw at the 99p Club... I saw a lot of shite ones.

JOHN AUSTIN: I still can't believe the Supernaturals didn't become superstars. They had two great singles, *Day Before Yesterday's Men* and *Smile* – you hear *Smile* on TV ads sometimes. But they were just an incredible fun band. The songs were good, solid pop, played like fuck – but it was the live show that got you. They'd just do whatever they liked. I remember one wee place in Edinburgh – all arches, but I can't remember its name. The piano player wasn't in the song, so he got up and started walking around with a stupid robot walk, keeping the beat of the song, going into the audience to drink people's pints... I think they kept swapping instruments all night as well. You just got this feeling of greatness off them. I wasn't surprised when they got signed, but I was surprised when nothing came of it.

CLAIRE SWEENEY: When the Note moved to King Street we started doing vegan-only food, so I think we got a reputation for being animal lovers and tree-huggers. One night, someone left their hamster there, with a wee note saying they couldn't look after it any more and could we find it a new home? Craig, the owner, could – he knew someone who specialised in caring for distressed hamsters, and the wee thing went away quite happily...

We gave Rolf Harris a Stylophone
Lies get out of hand for the Johnny Seven

AFTER the demise of Barky! Barky, Jim Brady and friends were looking round for something a little more sedate to do and settled on a very relaxing semi-retirement hobby easy-listening vibe. The plan was to have a few mates playing cheesy lounge tracks, and to do it drunk; but it was so successful that the Johnny Seven found themselves taking it a little further than they'd originally planned.

TAM: We did a demo and came up with the idea of having them numbered, but we realised everyone would want either 001 or 007, so we had fifty of each made up... Someone would say, 'I'd really like number 007.' And then we'd say, 'You're in luck, mate – I think we've still got that one...'

JIM: We set out to tell the biggest lies right from the start and everyone just embraced it. We went, 'We're all millionaires, we've been doing this for years and we wrote all the Bond themes.' Everyone from Mogwai to Belle and Sebastian were just like, 'Aye, you did!' But then they'd tell other people and it would become true...

TAM: We told people we'd done the music for the movie *Boxing Helena* – nobody was ever going to watch it so nobody knew it was shite. What we said, I mean, not the movie, although it was shite an'all... So they believed that too!

JIM: And we lived in a penthouse flat in the Merchant City, with a fire pole in the middle that we slid down to get to the Sevenmobile! John Williamson got us some amazing gigs – I don't know whether he was using us to take the piss out of other bands or just taking the piss out of us!

We supported Justin Currie – or Derek Amitri, to give him his Sunday name – and started getting album launches and the like. Rolf Harris asked us to support him when he had his hit with *Stairway to Heaven*. The crowd were insane and we couldn't hear ourselves, but when we played the final tune, the theme from *Star Trek*, we held up our Stylophones and the place nearly exploded! We had four and Rolf didn't have one, so we gave him one of ours...

TAM: That was the gig when Rolf was talking to us about how it was a shame that some kids didn't do anything with their hands nowadays. 'You can do plenty,' he said as a girl walked by. 'Like, play with that sheila's minge!' I don't think I've ever been more astonished in my life – except for when I heard Glen Michael from Cartoon Cavalcade say 'Bastard!' in a bookies...

Electric shock therapy
George Ross Watt to the rescue

JIMMY DEWAR, who'd been in Stone the Crows and Robin Trower's band, died in 2002 after a long illness. As well as having been close mates and bandmates with Frankie, he'd encouraged Scotland's biggest blues guitar legend, George Ross Watt, to get on out there.

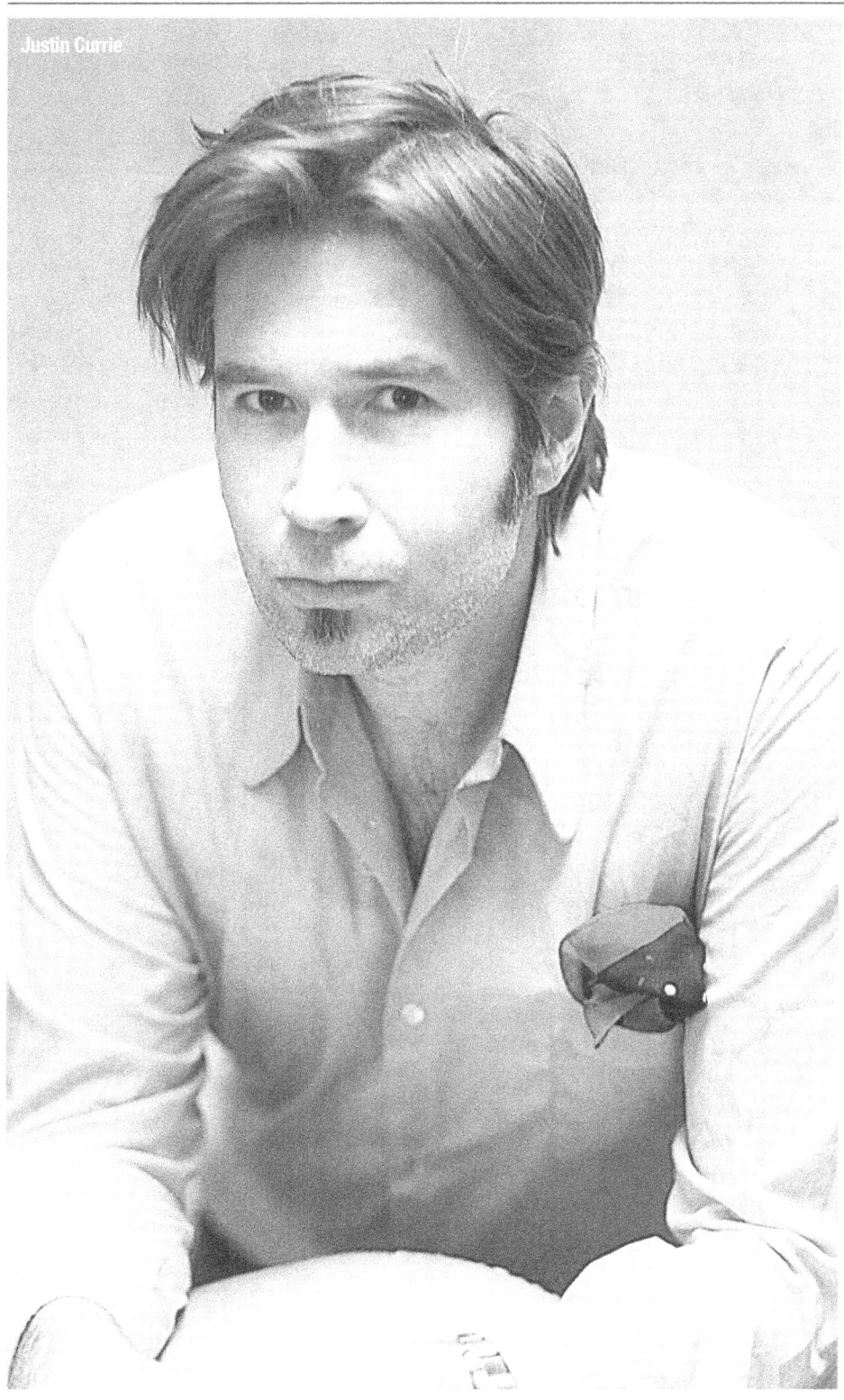

Justin Currie

SHIFTY, Big George and the Business: We got going after Jimmy had to stop gigging. He and Big George remained very close friends, and George conducted his funeral service.

He told a story about the night they'd finished a gig and gone back to Jimmy's for a wee refreshment. George went to put on a Ray Charles album, but Jimmy said, 'Frankie Miller's new album is there if you want to play it.' George said, 'I thought Ray was your favourite?' And Jimmy said, 'Well, to be honest, Frankie's the best singer I've ever heard – but don't you tell him that till after I'm dead, because you'll just give him a big heid.'

DAVE ARCARI: It was Big George who got me into music, guitars and blues. I used to join in with a country duo in the Ben Nevis BAR who encouraged me to grab the Tele and play some Dylan or whatever else I'd been learning. The guy on pedal steel was a complete alky – he was magnificent, but I could never work out how he could play so well and not be able to stand or speak...

One night they weren't there so as I wandered back towards Partick I saw there was live music in the Exchequer. Big George and Jimmy Dewar were on – I discovered the blues and it changed my life.

SHIFTY: We'd played just about everywhere so it was time to do an album. We went to Shabby Road Studios in Kilmarnock and it was recorded and mixed in just two days. Then there was a hefty delay in getting it mastered and pressed because one of the band had to be at the high court... So one night, a punter shouted, 'When's this alleged album coming out?' We didn't have a title up to then, so we called it *The Alleged Album*.

In keeping with the back-to-basics feel of the whole project, we ordered 1000 plain white covers, 2000 'Alleged Album' stickers – one for the front and one for the back – and 1000 inner sleeves. The band and crew then proceeded to insert discs into inners, inners into covers, and put stickers on the front and back. A few had squinty stickers and hidden messages to relieve the tedium. Then we hand-delivered them to local shops all over the place, and they sold out in the first few days. Fluff Freeman praised it on his Radio One rock show.

STEFF MILLS: They're alleged to have pulled a dead-wide trick to promote the album – they sent their mates into record shops to ask about it before it was out, so the owner wouldn't know anything about it. Then after there'd been a dozen people asking, the band would go in and say, 'Would you like to stock our album?' Course they would!

George, of course, is a legend. Among the many stories, lots of which seem to include shite, is my personal favourite, which goes like this. His rider is very simple – 'A bottle of

Southern Comfort whenever I shout for one' – and he'll happily down three during the course of an evening. One night he must have done unusually well, for he staggered into a taxi, bellowed, 'Bangkok, my man!' and feel asleep. The cab driver took him to Banknock and kicked him out.

SHIFTY: There was a short-circuit on stage once and I was electrocuted – I was flung across the stage and landed in the drumkit.

George realised what was happening and kicked the bass out of my grip, breaking the circuit. He came over to check I was alright and shouted for Richie the roadie to get me a treble Southern Comfort. Richie came back and George drank it... well, he'd had a stressful moment! I had burns on my hands but I was okay...

An insecurity of musicians
Salute to the life and times of a pub rock band

SCOTT PIRRIE: My contribution to the Scottish music scene was slight, probably to the point of insignificance. I started a band called the Answer in the unfashionable nineties, and for ten years or so we kicked around the pubs and clubs of the central belt, making no impact whatsoever.

There were thousands of bands like us – we were the guys no one quite remembered seeing, the forgettable first act on the three-band bill, the cannon fodder on the local scene, hanging around at the back of the dressing room full of awkward strangers. If they ever need a collective noun for musicians, I think it should be 'an insecurity'.

We had no business sense at all, save for blind enthusiasm, a modicum of talent and, like all the other hopefuls, a collective libido that required at least three trained handlers at times. But the small guys like us kept the whole machine in motion.

Of course, that's not to say we were in any way content with our lowly calling – it went without saying we'd have sold our grandmothers for the six-figure Sony deal, the tabloid courtship and the global female appreciation of our work.

Even though these things didn't happen, we still had a hell of a ride. From the unfettered enthusiasm of places like The Twa Corbies in Cumbernauld to the pretentious bollocks of King Tut's, our varied and sometimes itchy career included the inadvertent burning down of a night club in Blantyre, the electrocution of a guitarist, the loss of a perfectly good watch down a Cockermouth toilet, the loss of a perfectly good drummer in the Glasgow underground, enough chicken pakora to fill a small whaling trawler, three cylinder-head gaskets, one acrimonious divorce, one documented case of genital herpes and four chipped teeth – three due to the faithful old SM58 microphone and one due to a kebab.

I suppose at times I hated it then – but I long for it now. So this goes out to the wee fish that made the big pond all the more inviting, the Transit van sleepovers, the questionable underwear, the venues that ranged from the palatial to the downright infectious, the fights, the beer, the broken hearts. I'd recommend it to anyone.

In conclusion

JUSTIN CURRIE: Backstage we've been thanked for inventing golf. We've been invited to house parties where there was nobody there, no furniture, no food in the cupboards and no stereo. We've sat drunk in the back of strangers' pickup trucks and been taken, singing, to faraway suburbs where somebody's senile grandmother won't notice, to bars with no signs outside, pool halls full of insane rednecks, hotel rooms full of the wrong kind of people, the wrong kind of drugs and the wrong kind of music. We've woken up to find stowaways on the tour bus, all the furniture in our rooms gone, strange anonymous Polaroids of all sorts of sexual and chemical deviance pushed under our doors, and – most absurdly of all – we managed to sustain a mainstream career in the music business in the US and the UK on the thinnest of talents, the most meagre of ideas and the absence of cool.

God save rock'n'roll!

Also from Noisewave Publishing

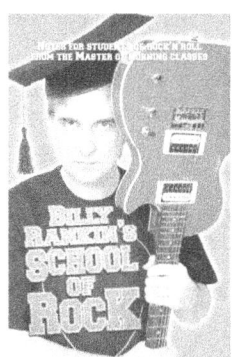
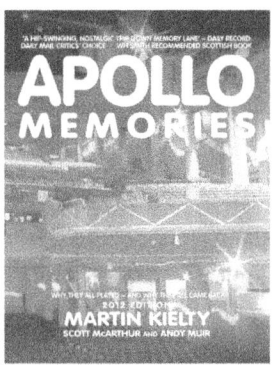
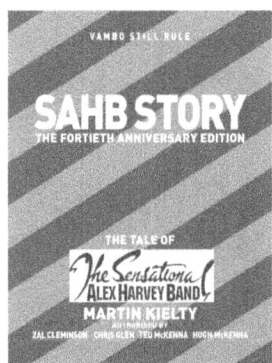
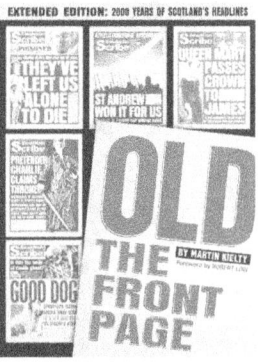

www.noisewave.co.uk

www.ingramcontent.com/pod-product-compliance
Lightning Source LLC
Chambersburg PA
CBHW080248200526
45166CB00021B/1104